Eight

The Book About Just One Chapter

G.D. Dowey

RIGHTEOUS⊶ACTS

Chapin, South Carolina

2020

ISBN 978-1-7359876-0-6
Library of Congress Control Number: 2020920348

This book is dedicated to
my brothers and sisters in Christ at FRESH Church.
We are the family of God.

Contents

Preface

When I was a young ministerial student, I heard my pastor refer to Romans 8 as an indispensable and central chapter to the life of the Christian. Intrigued, many times over the years I have read it, studied it, memorized sections of it, and taught and preached from it. Recently, after listening to Dr. Derek Thomas' lectures and studies on this chapter from 2019, I saw the critical need of our church to be reminded of a sound doctrine of soteriology and spiritual growth. So I led our church, preaching a series on the entire eighth chapter of Paul's letter to the Romans. My personal study of this major epistle has deepened my walk with the Lord Jesus, and I wanted our people to see and experience the same. God continues to use this study as He shapes us for the future of FRESH Church.

These chapters are taken from the sermon series, "Romans 8: The Greatest Chapter in the Bible." It was preached from the pulpit of Fresh Church. For fourteen weeks during the summer of 2020, right in the middle of the Coronavirus Pandemic, we delved intensely into this fantastic study. God blessed our church from it. Instead of giving in to the culturally correct thing to do at the time, which was teaching and preaching against the fear of COVID-19, we, instead, dug deep into God and His Holy Word.

There was a sense of sadness as we got near the end, knowing that we would be moving on to another series. Starting out, I made the statement, "Romans 8 may be the greatest chapter in the Bible!" When we finished, many believed with me that maybe it is, indeed. A careful and precise study of biblical theology is massively important for the Christ-follower. Texts like Romans 8 help us to understand who we were without Jesus, who we now are in Christ, and what we are becoming. In a culture that is fast intent on killing the church, it's time for believers to know exactly who we are in God. May the Holy Spirit take you further with Him as you commit to study His Word.

Greg Dowey
September 2020
Jekyll Island, Georgia

Chapter One

Romans 8: The Greatest Chapter in the Bible. Why? Because it's a precise chapter on how to live. In these extreme and kooky days that have brought about more confusion, we need clarity. Feeling more confined, we need to be loosed. Romans 8 proclaims our freedom in Christ. It reveals God's particulars about how He has planned life out for us… spiritually. Romans details to us how we are rescued by Christ, and how we are to grow in Him. I will not belabor the introduction because it's time to get down to business. Romans 8 has almost everything. Let's jump in, but begin slowly with one verse in this chapter, the first verse:

There is therefore now no condemnation
for those who are in Christ Jesus.
-Romans 8:1

In order to understand Romans 8:1, you have to understand Romans 7... and 6... and 5... and 4... and 3. Romans is Paul's masterpiece. He is moving along and in chapters three, four, and five he succinctly paints the picture of where we are. We are lost without Christ. He then goes on, in chapters six and seven, to illustrate how we feel, but comes back to this massive stroke of the pen in the opening of chapter eight. It's like a walk-off homerun type of a sentence. It's a game winning touchdown as time runs out. It's V-day. It's the drop the mic and walk off the stage line in the speech that everyone has been waiting for, but you didn't know it was coming. It's that type of a declaration. Why? At this point, hopefully you have read the Old Testament and some of the major themes:

- Adam and Eve
- Sin in the garden... nakedness
- Clothed by God, but tossed out
- The world gets worse: Noah
- Abraham: 100 years old, becomes a dad and father of many nations
- Isaac: Abraham's son

- Jacob: twelve sons; Joseph: coat, jealousy, sold into slavery
- Joseph interprets Pharaoh's dream and is put in charge
- Drought and famine; Joseph is the hero and moves his family to Egypt
- New Pharaoh doesn't care, and makes slaves of Joseph's family
- 430 years in captivity, and Moses delivers
- Moses is given the Ten Commandments
- Joshua leads God's people into the Promised Land
- The people cry for a King
- Saul, David, and Solomon
- The kingdom splits, and about nineteen kings each come to the throne over a period of five hundred years
- Silent period
- The New Testament

Paul takes all this history, all these happenings, all of God's men and women. The high points and the lows. He highlights the major ones and interprets them, gives their meaning, and then he applies it all. We arrive at the letter, the book to the church at Rome... Romans.

The next fourteen chapters will be spent in fantastic work, focusing primarily on chapter 8. Can I emphasize once more that this chapter is very important to the Christian? It's huge! Maybe this illustration will get to the point I am making:

On the night of April 18, 1775, hundreds of British troops set off from Boston toward Concord, Massachusetts, in order to seize weapons and ammunition stockpiled there by American colonists. Early the next morning, the British reached Lexington, where approximately seventy minutemen had gathered on the village green. Someone suddenly fired a shot – it's uncertain which side – and a melee ensued. When the brief clash ended, eight Americans lay dead and at least an equal amount were injured, while one redcoat was wounded.

The British continued on to nearby Concord, where that same day they encountered armed resistance from a group of patriots at the town's North Bridge. Gunfire was exchanged, leaving two colonists and three redcoats dead. Afterward, the British retreated back to Boston, skirmishing with colonial militiamen along the way and suffering a number of casualties; the Revolutionary War had begun.

The incident at the North Bridge was later memorialized by Ralph Waldo Emerson in his 1837 poem "Concord Hymn," whose opening stanza is:

By the rude bridge that arched the flood
Their flag to April's breeze unfurled
Here once the embattled farmers stood
And fired the shot heard round the world.

Romans 8. It's the shot heard around the world. It's the firing of God's message out into the Cosmos, into space, and onto Earth. To every created thing to hear and know…know what? This:

There is therefore now no condemnation
for those who are in Christ Jesus.

-Romans 8:1

Pastor Greg, why is this statement so important? Before Christ, we are condemned. There was no way for you and me to come out of the pit of destruction. We were helpless. Before Paul makes this charge, he explains the fighting that is done within us in chapters six and seven, and it all leads up to this fantastic truth. This is greater than a line from Braveheart! It's better than them raising Rudy on their shoulders after Notre Dame beats Georgia Tech! This is Rocky stuff! This is the dessert before the main course. It's the walk-off homerun where you leave the field, but Paul opens up with it here in Romans 8.

We weren't favored Jews. We are sinners, and God is righteous, so there is no hope. We were born sinners and so there was no shot for us… up until the truth in Romans 8:1. Paul is explaining how we, as Gentiles, have always been on God's mind. We are long lost family that have been given the opportunity to come home. And we need some type of explanation, some type of message, some type of understanding. That's what Romans is about, and then there is this opening statement, *"There is therefore now no condemnation for those who are in Christ Jesus."*

Let's begin with an outline of the importance of this first verse. There are four points here in this chapter but let me combine everything I want to say in the first three points, then I will talk about the significant last point. Let's put all of the bad news up front. It's only when you know the bad news that you can comprehend the good news of Jesus Christ. Here it is. Without Christ,

1. Everyone is in <u>Condemnation</u>
2. <u>Condemnation</u> leads to Confusion, Doubt, Confinement & Depression
3. <u>Condemnation</u> is synonymous with Hell

As you can tell, I always like to start with the bad news. I know what you are thinking, "I thought this was going to be a fun study?" Why has everyone been condemned? Because everyone is a sinner! Back in chapter three of Romans Paul is setting up this one verse we are looking at today. We are sinners by birth, and by nature… we are born into it. Sinners do the opposite of what God tells them – what to do and how to live. Condemnation is defined as *awaiting God's judgement*. Condemnation is also the complete opposite of justification (saved) with God. Without Christ we are living in guilt, shame, and sin. And, we don't have the means, strength, or power to get out of it.

> *Basically, all of us, whether insiders or outsiders, start out in identical conditions, which is to say that we all start out as sinners."*   *-Romans 3:9 MSG*

I regularly tell the congregation and church how important the Psalms are to our daily lives. I do it so often I sound like a broken record. Paul says everyone is a sinner. It's where we start out. Then, in summation by stringing Psalm 14, Psalm 53, Psalm 5; then Psalm 140, Psalm 10, and Psalm 36; then adding a few lines from Isaiah and Proverbs, Paul makes this statement… stirs it all together real good… it's like a batter that is poured into a pan, thrown into an oven at 350° with the timer set at 40 minutes, and when you take it out you have what I call a "Book of Romans Cake!" Here's the Psalm-inspired cake in Romans:

> *None is righteous, no, not one; no one understands; no one seeks for God. All*

have turned aside; together they have become worthless; no one does good, not even one... Their throat is an open grave; they use their tongues to deceive... The venom of asps is under their lips... Their mouth is full of curses and bitterness... Their feet are swift to shed blood; in their paths are ruin and misery, and the way of peace they have not known... There is no fear of God before their eyes. -Romans 3:10-18

None. Did you see that? No one seeks Him. I'm incapable, you are incapable. It means we can't get up out of the pit on our own no matter how hard we try. And it's not like we don't need a helping hand to get us started up out of there. No, we need a crane to lift us out. We have no energy to fight sin, apart from Christ. He has to do it for us... thus the Cross. This one point is countercultural to the modern church's seeker-service designed for spiritual seekers. We don't seek God, He seeks us!

An analogy for you: you don't need a parachute. Jesus is not your parachute to help you safely touch down. You have been shoved out of the plane and below you are flames of about 10,000° Fahrenheit, and you are traveling toward that fire at 500 mph. You don't need something that is just going to slow you down from hitting hell, you need an outright rescue.

And here's the deal: too many of us are content with slowly descending into the fire… living in a condemned state, when Christ has set you free. Chapters six and seven of Romans basically tell us that many of us still live in this state of confusion and guilt. We have, you have — *if* you have — placed your trust in Christ. Then you have essentially prayed or begged Him to save you, and He did. You pleaded with Him to rescue you… you may have even shed some tears. You experienced His salvation believing that He died for you, rose again, and is seated at the right hand of the Father. He took your sins away. But here's the problem of many: you sinned again, and you are confused about it. Wait a minute! Does that mean I am condemned again? Does it mean I was going to hell, then Jesus saved me and I was on my way to the good life, but then I sinned again so now I am lost again and on the way to hell again? No.

Here's what happens time and time again: we pray again, "God forgive me." And we feel cleansed, because we believe it, but then we sin again somewhere down the line, maybe even the next day or next minute, and we pray for salvation again. We are caught up in this perpetual cycle. And the result for many is that we quit church for a while because we don't feel worthy. We put our spiritual life on pause because we feel that we have disappointed God beyond repair. Paul says that is a problem… and it's a problem of our misunderstanding the magnificent power of God. It's a total failure to understand. So, Paul says it, and I have to shout it out by putting it in bold type because we just don't get it:

> *There is therefore now no condemnation*
> *for those who are in Christ Jesus.*
> *-Romans 8:1*

There is a conclusion here. *Therefore* is derived from what Paul has been saying in chapters six and seven. You are not perfect. Christ is perfect *for you*. Now, in chapters six and seven — and I believe also in three, four, or five — Paul says several times, "So, we go on sinning and living life like we want to… so that God can keep forgiving us? So… we assume that we need to do our part by keeping on sinning, so that grace will do its part?"

"NOOOOOOOOOOOO!" Paul says. You don't get it if you think that. You will continue to struggle… you will continue to sin if you believe that. But it says,

> *There is therefore now no condemnation*
> *for those who are in Christ Jesus.*
> *-Romans 8:1*

Yet there is still this depression there. It's human nature. It's the way we are wired. What do we do? Getting rid of spiritual depression requires us to say farewell, so long, bye-bye to our past. Christ died for your sins. Often we think back on how bad they were in the early church age and we think, "I'm just so bad, probably worse…." Hear this, God says: *I get it! I know! That's why I sent my Son! You can't do it. You need Him!* We are unable to keep the Law (Ten Commandments) that point to the way we should live. It's why I say we not only have to visit the Cross in our lives, we have to live there! We have to be reminded of His sacrifice, and the power of the Resurrection. We have to get on our knees there and live a life of continued confession. Do you get it yet? Again,

> *There is therefore now <u>no condemnation</u> for those who are in Christ Jesus.*
> *-Romans 8:1*

It says "NO condemnation." None. I think the major problem is that we don't fully appreciate and comprehend the *no* part. We are set free from our guilt, and we will talk about freedom when we look at verses 2-4. But there is also a power we have: we don't have to sin. How is it the super-spiritual Christian (you know that jerk) always wants to emphasize that we have the will to choose God, but they never mention we have the power of the Holy Spirit to not sin?

Paul builds up to this crescendo of sorts in chapter eight so that we see a once-and-for-all power here. Here's what it means: we are righteous sinners. Both. Righteous, and sinners. The two states exist simultaneously. Martin Luther said, "Simul Justus et Peccatore." It is Latin for *We are righteous, clean before God, while still a sinner.*

Without Christ we are condemned for sure, but the human feeling is that we are often confused people. It's a sociological fact. Confusion leads to chaos… it's the same as running around like chickens with their heads cut off. I know plenty of confused people today… don't you? We are certainly confused about the state of the world. When COVID-19 passes, there will be a line out the door waiting for the enemy to confuse things with something else, and to once again redirect life onto a path of chaos. Okay, here's the truth, and the good news we have been waiting for:

4. Those in Christ will not experience <u>Condemnation</u>

> *There is therefore now no condemnation*
> *for those who are in Christ Jesus.*
> *-Romans 8:1*

I just like re-emphasizing and repeating it. What else is there to say? You and I, those who are in Christ, are free and are not under the condemnation of the Law… meaning that we have been set free from sin and heaven awaits. If there were ever a time to say, "Hallelujah," it's now! Don't get sidetracked and stuck in some religious beliefs that have nothing to do with the grace of God. The Apostle Paul makes this massive declaration that you desperately need to memorize. We are free from sin and its destructive results, and we are free to live. Why aren't you living for Him? There is no excuse.

Moneyball is a movie about Billy Beane, the manager of the Oakland As, who is trying to assemble a winning team. Ultimately during the 2002 season, the Athletics win an unprecedented twenty consecutive games, setting the American League record. But despite all their success, the A's lose in the first round of the post-season.

As Beane sits alone and sullen in the clubhouse, the general manager attempts to convince him that he had "won pretty big." Then, seeing that Beane is unconvinced, the GM invites Beane to the video room. He has cued up a segment of tape for Beane to watch – a clip about a player named Jeremy Brown, a catcher from their minor league baseball team, the Visalia Oaks.

Here's what happens in that video: The catcher is at bat. He hits a fastball and sends it deep into center field. The catcher rounds first and is about to do what he's never done before. He's going to head to second. But he stops. He stops and crawls back to the security of first base. He clings to first base like a frightened child clings to a teddy bear. It's his nightmare. "They're laughing at him," says Beane. And they *were* laughing at him.

But the general manager explains why they're laughing at him. "Jeremy's about to find out why; Jeremy's about to realize that the ball went sixty feet over the fence. He hit a home run, and he didn't even realize it." Beane stares at the screen as Jeremy finally discovers that the ball went out of the park and then jubilantly rounds the bases for home.

This is a picture of what Romans 8:1 tells us. We don't have to cling to first base. Christ has already hit the home run that brings us home. Hallelujah! We haven't been paying attention or realized the fullness of the Truth of God. His righteousness has been credited to our account, and we are now at peace with God. We don't have to live in fear carefully crawling back to, and then clinging to, first base. Instead, we can jubilantly run the bases as we head confidently toward home. If your life is stalled at first, second, or even third, then realize Jesus has already hit the homerun and you weren't even on base! He hit it for you and now you and I just need to run. Here's the recap just once more: *"There is therefore now no condemnation for those who are in Christ Jesus."*

Did you hear what Paul declares in Romans 8:1? You are FREE!

Chapter Two

Years ago, I sat in the electric chair. It was the actual electric chair the state of South Carolina once used for the purpose of electrocuting those on death row. During that era, at the appointed time, murderers were granted a last meal and a visit from family and clergy, then were led down the hall to the chair. They would shave the killer's head and legs and apply a gel that would facilitate a quicker death. The chair was named Ol' Sparky.

That old wooden death seat was worn out. It had weathered leather straps to hold arms and legs down, and the buckles were rusted. I could see the lever across the room on the wall that triggered the electrical currents, where they would switch it up to bring down the high voltage. I hadn't planned on sitting in the chair that day, but the man giving me the tour offered me the opportunity. It's a good thing my wife didn't know I sat in it… I don't think she would have liked it. It's a *great* thing there weren't any former deacons or disgruntled church members there, because they may well have flipped the switch! I'm sure I have some enemies who are reading now and saying, "Oh, I wish I had been there!"

An important question for you this morning is this: Would you have sat in that chair? Hey, it was harmless, even though a little unnerving for me. Neither the Warden nor the Executioner were there, so that calmed my nerves. Many would say, "NOOOOOOOOO! No way. I'm not sitting in that thing!"

I've got tough news for some of you today folks: for those who are not in Christ, *you are not free*. You *do* sit in an electric chair. If you are not a Christ-follower, then you stand on that platform with the hangman's noose around your neck. Your head is in the guillotine. Your body is strapped down on the gurney with the needle in your arm connected to that bag of a mixed cocktail bag of poison, and the executioner is ready to perform his duty. The Bible is clear. Those without Christ are facing a not-so-good forever ending.

In chapter one, we learned that *there is therefore now no condemnation for those who are in Christ Jesus*. But – if you're not in Christ Jesus, you are awaiting the judgement of eternal death.

Here's where this chapter talks to you and me: We are in a prison of guilt and shame without Christ. Our every move is determined by the warden, and his name is sin. Prison seems to be the backdrop of Paul's latter years. He wrote several of his letters from prison. He contrasted freedom with the penal institution. He commented and remarked on the days he spent in dungeons. But they were no big deal to Paul, it seems. He tells us what real freedom is like, yet he was in jail.

Think about it. Of all the positions God could have put Paul in to explain to us about the beautiful relationship with Christ, He lets the penitentiary be the background. God didn't make the background a serene field of roses or the gentle winding of a river through a stunning garden. God, in His brilliance, is spot-on with putting Paul – the greatest theological mind ever, the greatest God-mind ever – in jail, handcuffed and shackled to a guard 24/7, to explain freedom to us. He does it, remember, because we are in sin-prison without Jesus. Sin tells us when to eat, what to eat, and relishes in ordering us around. I really don't think we understand that sometimes. Understand, there was no due process for Paul… he didn't know from day to day if he was going to live or die. Yet, he was free.

My wife, Missie, and I were watching a TV show the other evening and it told a story about a man named Archie Williams who was falsely accused and convicted of rape in 1982 and put in prison for 37 years. He was not guilty, and after one of those pro-bono goodwill attorney organizations took up his case and proved by DNA that he didn't do it, he was released. That story was on the popular reality television show, *America's Got Talent*. Believe me, the guy could sing! It was an incredible story. How do you do thirty-seven years with that great attitude? How do you get through something like that? The answer: he was free in his heart and mind even though imprisoned and restricted by bars.

And maybe you would complain today about being in a prison of fear, or a prison of condemnation, or a prison of suffering, or a prison of doubt, and you would say, "I didn't do it, I don't belong here, I didn't do anything to deserve this!" Yeah you did. You and me both.

I'll remind you we are in Romans 8, in a study through this fantastic chapter in the middle of the New Testament and, as I've said, maybe the greatest chapter in the Bible. Heading into Romans 8, Paul explains to us how God has freed us:

> *For the law of the Spirit of <u>life has set</u>*
> *<u>you free in Christ Jesus</u> from the law of sin*
> *and death. For God has done what the*
> *law, weakened by the flesh, could not*
> *do. By sending his own Son in the*
> *likeness of sinful flesh and for sin, he*

condemned sin in the flesh, in order that the <u>righteous requirement of the law</u> might be fulfilled in us, who walk not according to the flesh but according to the Spirit. -Romans 8:2-4

In July 1976, one hundred and three Jewish hostages were taken by terrorists in Entebbe, Uganda. An Air France Jet was highjacked and the non-Jews were set free. After a week's planning, a 90-minute rescue operation plan was hatched. Israel secretly sent their commandos into Entebbe to free their people. It was called Operation Entebbe. Idi Amin, an evil dude, was the president of Uganda.

The problem was tremendous. How do they free 103 of their own people from seven terrorists? Their plan was simple. They entered the area where the hostages and terrorists were together and shouted in Hebrew, *"GET DOWN NOW, CRAWL!"* Since the terrorists didn't understand Hebrew and all the Jewish citizens did, they simply shot everyone still standing after they yelled this! It was a great escape story! All seven terrorists were killed, and all one hundred and three Jewish hostages were freed. Only two Jews were hit during the firing, one because he hesitated to obey, the other because he stood back up too soon. As we look at Romans 8:2-4, compare these things with Operation Entebbe.

- The hostages were unable and <u>incapable</u> of helping themselves

Freedom came because trained commandos came to their rescue, defeating their captors. Likewise, we are powerless, incapable of being set free or freeing ourselves from the prison and death sentence of sin. Oh, but Christ came to set us free and has completely defeated Satan through the cross.

- The <u>plan</u> was daring: Commandos risked their lives

God's plan was even more daring. Jesus came to die in our place. On the cross, Jesus took our sin upon Him and paid the death penalty in our place. It was a bold plan. Satan fell for it and thought he had won, but God had also planned the resurrection. Death could not hold Jesus and Satan was defeated so that we might be free.

- There were <u>simple</u> instructions

Everyone heard the words *"Get down now, crawl!"* Only those who did as they were told were rescued. Similarly, God's call goes out to those held captive in sin: *"Believe upon the Lord Jesus Christ and you shall be saved."* Everyone who listens to God's word and calls upon Him will be saved – will be rescued.

- Having been <u>set free</u> the hostages lived as free men

Can you even imagine any of the 103 hostages refusing to return to their families, or demanding that they remain in their place of captivity? Likewise, as Christians we, too, are to live in freedom. Unfortunately, though Christ has set us free we continue to live in bondage.

Many, many don't know what it means to be free because they haven't grasped their imprisonment in this life. Could it be that many church folks today think they have been cleared of their crimes, when in fact they have merely talked themselves into a sort of religious parole? Religious parole is living in the prison of guilt, shame, and spiritual poverty six days a week, but then on Sunday feeling all good inside because of the day off, or because you like the music, or because you can take a long walk, be with the family, go to brunch, or you can go to a church service. But when the lights go out on Sunday evening, it's roll call for the Monday grind. Laboring relationships and burdensome obligations are your security guards. You start stressing and complaining and acting like you live in jail.

Listen to this: Christianity is filled with people that erroneously believe just parts of God's Word. The reason is because they want to believe just enough so that they can feel good about everything. Let this sink in: <u>God always wounds before He heals</u>. All of us need to be wounded, to be humbled, because pride is inherent. It's a double-edged sword. We need to be right before God, but God gets to the heart of the matter and many times that hurts. A true relationship with Jesus exposes the dark cellars of sin's imprisonment. The trouble we get in today, the reason the church world is in the shape it's in today, is because of a simple lack of faith and trust in God and knowing what God's Word says.

What is lack of faith? The opposite of faith is reasoning too much. If you believe only what you can understand, then I doubt you know Christ. If you believe social media above the Word of God, you've got serious relationship problems with Jesus. Who can understand this mysterious God we serve without faith, without trust? It's faith, and faith alone, that saves us. Many church people have devised for themselves a personal theology of God – not based on the Bible but on their experiences, and what their friends say, and what Facebook and Twitter say. They have placed a higher value on regularity and dependability than they have on fidelity. In other words we may say out loud that God is good, and that Jesus came to die on the Cross, but we distance ourselves from repentance.

Quitting sin, *living a holy life*, *humbling ourselves* and *serving others* while considering them better than us, *give until it hurts*, and *go* even if it doesn't make sense. "No" we say, "I don't understand and I'm not taking part in something I don't understand."

Here's the real question ...

How, then, does Christ set us free?

We are free in Christ, but how does He set us free? The Gospel of John answers that question, in the most famous verse in his Gospel.

> *For God so loved the world, that he gave his only Son, that whoever believes in him should not perish but have eternal life.*
> *-John 3:16*

He had only one begotten Son, but He sent Him to die on a cross in order to save everyone who believes in Him. The Son would be "lifted up," John says, lifted up on a cross, exposed in public shame, hanging between heaven and earth, under the judgment of God against our sins – so that those who believed in Him should not perish but have everlasting life. Here's what this chapter is saying to us:

- Jesus took our place of Condemnation

But now the righteousness of God has been manifested apart from the law, although the Law and the Prophets bear witness to it—the righteousness of God through faith in Jesus Christ for all who believe. For there is no distinction: for all have sinned and fall short of the glory of God, and are justified by his grace as a gift, through the redemption that is in Christ Jesus, whom God put forward as a <u>propitiation</u> by his blood, to be received by faith.   -Romans 3:21-25

Oh, these verses are hated by modern so-called Christians. Why? Because there's not enough of sweet, sugary, syrupy love. We gravitate towards the love verses of the Bible not knowing that true love was given to us on a bloody Roman gibbet. Jesus died because He had to in order to fulfill God's covenant.

Jesus Christ is able to set us free because He has dealt with the sin that enslaves us — that put us in that prison of guilt, shame, doubt, and negativity. We can never atone for our own sin… we can never pay for our own sins. We can never break its power. We can never come to God and say, *"God, surely what I have done is enough to compensate for my sins. I've given to the poor, I've helped put a roof on a house in the*

Caribbean, and I've been nice and kind and worn a mask throughout this Pandemic!" Nothing we can do can possibly compensate for our sin.

Most of the book to the Galatians is about this subject. But God sent His own Son – think of it, *His own Son* – who stood in for us, in our place. Since He had no sins of His own to atone for, He was qualified to make a sacrifice for our sins. He lived a perfect life. He showed us how to live, before He went to the Cross to die for us. This is a good point, write it down: <u>Jesus came to show us how to live, before He died for us</u>. Again, no sacrifice we could make could ever be adequate to atone for sin. But He was able and willing to do it. Because of that, we can be set free from guilt and from the bondage it creates. Propitiation is the requirement for payback. Propitiation is that fantastic religious word meaning to satisfy. Jesus death on the Cross satisfied God's wrath, in other words, paid for our sins.

- Jesus reveals our place in Him

Christ also sets us free in another way: through the truth about God – and about ourselves – that He reveals. If we believe in Him, we will come to know the truth, and the truth will set us free. That is His promise.

I have met some exceptionally intelligent people who cannot understand the Christian gospel. They hear its message as if it were a lecture on morality. Yet the gospel is not difficult to understand, it's simple. Simple enough for even a child Jesus says. If we can't explain the Gospel to a five-year-old, then we don't understand it ourselves. The problem lies within us — in our spiritual blindness. It's not being smarter than others but understanding the blessing of God by faith in Him. <u>If there is resistance in the heart to *loving* God, there will be resistance in the mind to *knowing* God— and therefore to listening to and seeking God</u>. Only the truth can set us free. Jesus is able to set us free because of who He is and because of what He shows us.

Chapter Three

John Chrysostom, the greatest preacher of the Fourth Century, had the entire book of Romans read to him once a week. Augustine, Luther, and John Wesley all came to faith in Christ due to the book of Romans. Romans is the fullest, grandest, most comprehensive statement of the Gospel. When you read the Old Testament and then the Gospels, the book of Acts, and then Romans, you say, "Oh yeah! Now I get it!" Romans is like a coiled spring. When it is loosed, it leaps and jumps through the mind and heart to shape our horizon and our life. It's that important. It makes that much sense.

You know what doesn't make sense? That during the Coronavirus pandemic there are no sports to watch on TV. Because of COVID, March Madness, the opportunity for the Lady Gamecocks to win the National Championship, and the Masters tournament were all canceled. The NBA and MLB shortened their seasons without fans in the stands. Then they opted to do the sports seasons with cardboard cutouts and piped in screaming fans. The NFL did the same and just continued to suffer with their own internal problems. There have been a few NASCAR races without spectators... but it's not the same. Nuts isn't it? But, that's not the craziest thing I've seen through all of this.

One night a few weeks into the pandemic I was flipping through the channels, hoping that there would a game on, although I knew there was not... that makes no sense either. So, since there are millions and millions of taped baseball, basketball, and football games, it would make sense to air some and let us relive the glory days, right? Right! So, they did that with the Atlanta Braves and their glory years of the 1990's. And then... and then... and I'm not lying... I tuned in one evening... we were still in COVID crisis and lockdown, mind you... and as I tuned in to Atlanta Braves baseball, there was a rain delay! Do you get what I'm saying? I shot up out of bed! "This can't be happening! Am I dreaming?" It's the one thing that you can't stand when it's live and real, but when there is game after game after game to choose from, the producers choose a rain delay? What happened? The producers weren't paying attention and just picked an old game to run and didn't take into account that there may be a rain delay. So many things in our world don't make sense these days, but maybe it's because someone has not been attentive enough.

Understand this: Romans makes perfect sense, and God wants our full attention. To seek after God, after He has sought us, takes careful attention. In the very first verse of the very first chapter in Romans Paul says it's God's Gospel, and God's Gospel is about God. Now let's look at the verses for our study:

> *For those who live according to the flesh set their minds on the things of the flesh, but those who live according to the Spirit set their minds on the things of the Spirit. For to set the mind on the flesh is death, but to set the mind on the Spirit is life and peace. For the mind that is set on the flesh is hostile to God, for it does not submit to God's law; indeed, it cannot. Those who are in the flesh cannot please God*   *-Romans 8:5-8*

How often do you think about pleasing God? I mean, do you wake up each day and say to yourself, "Well, today is Wednesday, I have to go to work, I have some errands to run, and then there's the gym. Oh yeah, I need to run by Walmart and then by Publix before I prepare dinner. And, I almost forgot, I really need to do some things today that please God. After all, He has been pretty good to me." I would say most people never entertain that thought or allow those words to pass through their heads.

Romans 8:5-8 are sensible words, true words. They are words you and I need to adhere to and let your life be pleasing to God. Be attentive and understand what Paul is *not* saying... he is not saying that if you do these things, then you will live. Are you awake? He's *not* saying that. He is saying if you live in Christ, then you will do these things. Deep stuff isn't it? Pleasing God is simply obeying God. As we look at an important part of Scripture in Romans 8, what are the signs of a true work of God? It's not how much fruit do I have to produce, to demonstrate or prove that I am a Christian...no that's legalism, or trying to work your way into the good grace of God. Our question should be, "what do I get to do that is pleasing to God?"

There are at least 4 things Paul wants us to know here:

- The Christian is surely <u>ALIVE</u>!

Or, is the flesh alive in you? It's an easy litmus test. It's an easy evaluation. All Paul is doing here in verse 5 is distinguishing between two worlds. Look at it:

*For those who live according to the flesh
set their minds on the things of the flesh,
but those who live according to the Spirit
set their minds on the things of the Spirit.*
*   -Romans 8:5*

You see, it's easy for us to identify the flesh. We just look at our hand… there it is… the flesh… and all that comes with it. The word flesh means your mind, my mind, and whatever our minds lead us to do that gratify us, and us above anyone or anything else. A Christian, however, pronounces death to the flesh and God announces life. A Christian is someone who says, "Sin is killing me, so I need to kill sin." In other words, you can't live in two worlds. Stop trying, because only the miserable survive. Yet people try it all of the time. It's called hypocrisy. You say one thing and do another, you do one thing and say another. Paul has already addressed this in Romans 7. That's where he is, he says. So, we must live in the spirit.

*We are not sinners because we sin, we sin
because we are sinners.*
*   -RC Sproul (via Twitter)*

What is the spirit? In John 3, Nicodemus, a teacher – a rabbi – finds Jesus at night… and a hushed tone is the backdrop. He says quietly, *"Teacher, we know you have come from God, that's a definite! We see all these signs, all these miracles."* And to keep things on track – Jesus' track that is – Jesus switches gears on Nicodemus out of the blue, *"Truly Nick, if you are not born again you will not see the kingdom of God."* Nicodemus responds, *"How? How can a man be born again?"* What Jesus is saying is that it must be from above. It's outside of our ability. It's alien. We can't do it! It's the Spirit of God.

And that's the difficulty today in this world. We've created this mass confusion thinking that it's incumbent on us to intellectually, emotionally, and spiritually tap into this higher power called God. Most people incorrectly believe that we all have this built-in mechanism that is wired for an obligatory search for the Almighty. That's not true. That search comes with our belief that in order for us to know God we have to feel it first. And, if you don't feel it then you aren't getting it. No. That's not true. It's God who makes us alive.

It's interesting to note that Nicodemus was a religious teacher, a teacher of the Law, meaning that he knew the Old Testament like the back of his hand. And yet he didn't know how to come to God.

It pains me to say it, but it shows us today that there are many preachers and teachers, missionaries, and Christian professors who have no idea of what we are talking about today in Romans 8. Many teach about God, know about God, but not many teach, preach and live that God is alive. The Christian, the Christ-follower, the one that bows to Him, acknowledges Him... he/she becomes alive when God makes him/her alive. In other words, Nicodemus, your mindset is on the flesh.

You see, the Christian is alive to God and dead to the flesh. If we think we can turn our life on and off to Christ whenever we want to, then we are not obedient to God. We are just curious. We want to know without being obligated to follow. We want to be informed, but not to be involved. It's not like studying Latin at Harvard, it's not Greek at Oxford... look at it again:

> For to set the mind on the flesh is death, but to set the mind on the Spirit is life and peace.   -Romans 8:6

It's all in how you think! It's all in how you set your mind. Jesus tells us to repent and repent means to change your mind.

I was putting a TV dinner in the microwave the other day, and I had to set the timer. I had to program the correct time in, as I'm sure you know because you have a microwave also. Push "Cook Time," set the allotted minutes and seconds, then push "Go." The Christian life isn't that automatic, nor is your holiness. It's not setting the correct time and presto, you have your cake. We don't pray a little prayer and bam, instant gratification in the Lord. In other words, cooking up right living takes time. It's like baking the cake in an oven for an hour, only after you have done all of the prep-work, mixed it up, and figured out the time. How can I set my mind on life in the Spirit? Here's how:

- Hang around Christians
- Ask others to pray for your spiritual growth
- Look for examples from those Christians that live for Him
- Live! Quit sitting and soaking up more and more
- Give
- Serve
- Study the Word of God
- Lead others in the ways of righteousness
- In other words, the Christian Lives for God

There is fruit. There is love, joy, peace, patience, kindness, goodness, faithfulness, gentleness, self-control. There is giving, there is serving – there is giving and serving! There is going and inviting. There is *hilarious* giving. There is confidence, boldness, and hopefulness! That is where your mind is! It demonstrates those things because those are the things you concentrate on and move your mind towards. I always regretted it when I was a teenager and I announced I was going to a movie with my friends, because my dad would always respond, "You are warping your mind." It was his way of saying, "Garbage in, garbage out."

You see, in Romans 8, Paul is making it super simple for us. You either live for yourself, or you live for God. If you live for yourself then life is your own personal museum and you take daily tours, admiring yourself. Let me ask you a very important question… if we could take a ten-minute stroll through your mind, what would we find? A mind centered on the things of God, or a mind wishing you had more? A mind of pure thoughts and godly desires or a mind of squalor and ugliness? And you say, "Ha, Pastor, that's stupid, you can't walk through someone's mind!" Good point. Will you let us walk through your house? Can we go to your man-cave or she-shed? Can we look in your desk drawer? Let me simplify it even more, can we look at your debit card statement? Just a quick look, that's all. Will you list your last ten purchases for your church friends to see?

When I was in the Holy Land the last time my friends Don Kenney, John Herrin, and I were shopping in a Jewish jewelry store and I bought a silver medallion with the *Shema* on it. As John and I were talking I was explaining to him about Deuteronomy 6, and the owner of the store interrupted us and said, *"You are almost right."* It turns out I was mispronouncing *"Shema."* And I was only half right in my interpretation. There's nothing more embarrassing than being a preacher and corrected (twice!) about your understanding of the Bible in front of one of your churchgoers. This is the Shema:

> *Hear, O Israel: The Lord our God, the Lord is one. You shall love the Lord your God with all your heart and with all your soul and with all your might.*
> *-Deuteronomy 6:4*

I said, *"The meaning of Shema is 'hear.'"* And I was right, but… it's not just to hear by processing the words. Rather it means to hear and understand. It's deeper. If you understand something, especially God's Word, then you do something, or you apply it to your life.

Jesus was being peppered with rapid fire questions from the Sadducees and the Pharisees. They asked Him about money, they asked Him about the Resurrection, and then this smarty pants attorney pipes up,

> *And one of them, a lawyer, asked him a question to test him. "Teacher, which is the great commandment in the Law?" And he said to him, "You shall love the Lord your God with all your heart and with all your soul and with all your mind. This is the great and first commandment. And a second is like*

36

it: You shall love your neighbor as yourself. On these two commandments depend all the Law and the Prophets.
-Matthew 22:36-40

Hey folks, it's huge, it's important that we learn these verses, now more than ever. It is massive that we treat everyone with love and respect. I'm all for it. I've gone overboard as a Christ-follower to do regular inventory on my behavior to everyone, but understand this, hear this, hear this O Israel, hear this O America — what is the greatest commandment? Which one is first? To love the Lord God with all you have. It's missing from our American marketplace, it's missing from our American government, it's missing from our American education and institutions, it's missing from our neighborhoods, it's missing from our churches, and it's missing from many Christ-followers.

Oh yeah, we are all about turning over a new leaf today, aren't we? It's great that our eyes are being opened about racism, social justice, politics, and treating and loving our neighbors with respect. But, let me ask you: other than lip service... what are you giving to God? What are you lending and supplying to the cause of love, of love in Jesus Christ? Other than a few mumbling words of "Amen" or "Thank God," what have you given our Sovereign King? Have you given Him your life? If you have then you live for Him, and all of your life is His!

- The Christian Life is undoubtedly <u>Peace</u>

…but to set the mind on the Spirit is life and <u>peace</u>. For the mind that is set on the flesh is hostile to God, for it does not submit to God's law; indeed, it cannot.
-Romans 8:6,7

The very first thing that happens to people who become Christians is that they begin to think straighter.
-Martin Lloyd-Jones

Listen to me here: you are not going to suddenly feel it one day and come to Christ. Most likely, you will not be watching a movie on TV or playing golf and then suddenly say, "I need Jesus!" Paul addresses the mind, because it's in our mind where we win the battle with sin. Do you get it when I say it's God who does it? God rescues you. God saves you, not you! *He* does it. Our response is to change our mind. That is what repentance is. And when we do, when we give it to Him – here it is – there is peace. There is no doubt that the thing you need most of all in this life on a daily basis is peace. Peace like a river, as the hymn writer says. Peace that surpasses all understanding, as Paul says in Philippians 4.

Because of the iniquity of his unjust gain I was angry, I struck him; I hid my face and was angry, but he went on backsliding in the way of his own heart. I have seen his ways, but I will heal him; I will lead him and restore comfort to him and his mourners, creating the fruit of the lips.
"Peace, peace, to the far and to the near," says the Lord, "and I will heal him. But the wicked are like the tossing sea; for it cannot be quiet, and its waters toss up mire and dirt. There is no peace," says my God, "for the wicked."   -Isaiah 57:17-21

When God rescues you, He begins to heal your broken heart. Not only is salvation from above, but this restoration from the war you have been having within yourself all these years begins to calm, and God does indeed make your paths straight. It's the beginning of peace.

- The Christian is indisputably Spiritually minded

Here's the question: What does the HOLY SPIRIT think about? What's on His mind? Of course, the things of God.

Puritan preacher John Owen wrote on the subject of being spiritually minded. Owen, explaining how to know if you are going the right direction in your relationship with God, asked, "What does your mind default to?" When you are just relaxing, trying to rest, and taking your mind off of the distressful times, where does your mind automatically go? That is a sure sign of where your heart is, and where it is heading.

A unified heart and mind come only when we submit to Jesus as King in our lives. Stop dividing the two and bring them together in Jesus name.

Chapter Four

Satan continues his efforts to make sin less offensive, heaven less appealing, hell less horrific, and the Gospel less urgent. The world is in an uproar and there's no end in sight for those without Christ, unless they turn to Him. But for those in Him… the end is good. There are many movements, but it's only the Gospel that can truly end hatred in the hearts of sinners. Neither the US government, the Chinese communist party, nor the World Health Organization have any answer for the sinful soul. No one is born a Christian, the flesh cannot produce new life. Let's look at this passage of Scripture for today. This is a message series on the marvelous and superb letter of Paul that is called "Romans."

Those who are in the flesh cannot please God. You, however, are not in the flesh but in the Spirit, if in fact the Spirit of God dwells in you. Anyone who does not have the Spirit of Christ does not belong to him. <u>But if Christ is in you</u>, although the body is dead because of sin, the Spirit is life because of righteousness. If the Spirit of him who raised Jesus from the dead dwells in you, he who raised Christ Jesus from the dead will also give life to your mortal bodies through his Spirit who dwells in you. -Romans 8:8-11

Four Kinds of People:

#1 People who know they are not Christians
#2 People who are (saved) Christians, and they know it
#3 People who are saved, but not sure
#4 People who are not Christians, but believe they are

Category #2 is where you want to be. The most pathetic bunch is #4. Why do they believe they are Christians, but really aren't? How is it that they believe everything is okay between them and God? It's because they don't deal with sin. And in this crazy

42

world, that's not hard to understand. The contemporary church is in contempt of God. They are selling a cheap gospel that is being scarfed up by the lost. All you have to do, they say, is to "ask Jesus to come into your heart" and you're in!

Last week, I sent my son three books on motivation and leadership. They are classics. After he reads those, I'm sending him three more that I already have in mind. I want him to be successful and to know what true success entails. Why? Because there are myriad of so-called leaders and they are leading people to hell. They preach a popular message of hope and "everything is going to be all right," and it sounds good, but it's not.

Capitalistic Americans are hungry for motivation to win and to be successful. All of us are, to some degree. All of us want more than what we have, whether we admit it or not – and despite our efforts of altruism. Not only that, but we want to come by it as easily as possible. We avoid the important subject – the talk or introspection about our wickedness toward a Holy God. We are into pleasure seeking and pain avoiding.

The days of this calendar year have been the absolute worst on record for anyone breathing today. However, 2020 has been the greatest growing-time ever for the Christ follower. Ever! Life has been way too easy for people up until this year. Church also, has been too easy. We have put in a little bit of hard work, and we get a few breaks, and "Viola!" we are on Easy Street. We go to church every now and then. We like the cool music, we're able to be ourselves nowadays with casual dressing and wearing jeans. We give a little, we pray a little, and we endure someone preaching a little. Life and work are sort of the same. We get up on Mondays, go to the office for 8 hours, and wait for hump day. Sometimes the weekend arrives early... and then the party starts.

We've morphed our lives into these private little communities with our friends and technology and little party gatherings, and we just thought that this was going to be the norm forever. 2020 has served to wake us up to reality. The church needs to wake up, too. I've got bad news hot off the press today: we ain't – you ain't – going back to the good ole days. God has your attention now, so you better listen to Him. It's time to sit up straight and let God do business in your life.

Romans 8 is exactly for you – look back at this:

> _But if Christ is in you,_ although the body is dead because of sin, the Spirit is life because of righteousness.

Before "<u>But if Christ is in you</u>" many need to deal with "But what if Christ is NOT in you." If you doubt your relationship with Christ today... if because of today's circumstances in our world you have just taken inventory of your life and found that "Uh-oh, I may not be a Christian," here's why: We don't deal with sin. Everybody is good at pushing stuff under the rug. Everybody is good at procrastination. Everybody is good at "I'll do it tomorrow" when it comes to dealing with sin. Some want to act like they don't even know what the definition of sin means.

You may be a Christian, and I mean a fantastic one. I mean a true God-seeker. I mean the one that itches to get up every morning to serve and please God. The one that knows the Word of God because they spend time in it. The one that serves, gives, and has a wonderful attitude of love towards everyone. You forgive, you bless others, and you are the beacon of light in this dark world. Let me ask you a very important question: what do you do about sin? Understand, everyone has to deal with sin. If you don't, sin will deal with you. We need a mind that aims to kill... kill sin within ourselves.

The Mindset of Being Mortified

- There is sin to be dealt with, deal with it

  But I need something more! For if I know the law but still can't keep it, and if the power of sin within me keeps sabotaging my best intentions, I obviously need help! I realize that I don't have what it takes. I

45

can will it, but I can't do it. I decide to do good, but I don't really do it; I decide not to do bad, but then I do it anyway. My decisions, such as they are, don't result in actions. Something has gone wrong deep within me and gets the better of me every time. It happens so regularly that it's predictable. The moment I decide to do good, sin is there to trip me up.

-Romans 8:17-21

We have a tendency to avoid the subject of sin due to embarrassment. We should be embarrassed, in that it is gross rebellion and rejection of our holy God. Yet, the truth of the matter of sin is that all have run from God, hidden from God, and mutinied against His good will for our lives. Somebody said that the greatest testimony is that person that is not ashamed to use their past failures and sin to teach others to avoid it.

How do I deal with sin?
Say "NO" to it

For the grace of God has appeared, bringing salvation for all people, training us to renounce ungodliness and worldly passions, and to live self-controlled, upright, and godly lives in the present age, waiting for our blessed hope, the appearing of the glory of our great God and Savior Jesus Christ....

-Titus 2:11-13

Here are some more ways to further deal with it:

- Don't be content with Partial Holiness
- Kill it at its source – the Mind
- Be accountable to others
- Don't fall into legalism
- Foster and grow a desire to deal with sin
- Make seeking Him a priority until it becomes passion

Folks, here's the bottom line: the chief goal of the Christian life is righteousness.

> *If people really see that Christ has removed the fear of punishment from them by taking it into Himself, they won't do whatever they want, they'll do whatever He wants.*   *-John Bunyan*

In our desire to serve Him, to love Him and to draw to Him, there is a corresponding desire to deal with the sin our lives.

- There is now the ability to deal with sin

They loved Jesus' blessings. They loved Jesus' miracles. They loved Jesus' bread. They loved it that He turned water in wine. They loved Him feeding them fish and chips. However, they hated His words.

Christ offends America. Why has God been driven from the government and the schools? Why are the Ten Commandments removed from public places? Why is Christianity being labeled more and more a hate group? Sinful people hate holiness, and anything associated with it. As things change in this world, we have to stand up first and foremost for the Gospel. Even if it means we will lose church members, lose friends, or if it means discovering those who thought they were Christians but were really not. Christ offends people in this world because the Gospel is intolerant of sin. Oh… but the good news: Jesus took all of our sins and nailed them to the Cross.

Therefore, as one trespass led to condemnation for all men, so one act of righteousness leads to justification and life for all men. For as by the one man's disobedience the many were made sinners, so by the one man's obedience the many will be made righteous. Now the law came in to increase the trespass, but where sin

increased, grace abounded all the more, so that, as sin reigned in death, grace also might reign through righteousness leading to eternal life through Jesus Christ our Lord.
                                     -Romans 5:18-21

We now have the ability to deal with sin whereas once, before Christ, before the Cross of Christ, and before the Resurrection from the dead, we didn't. Before God sent His Son to deal with sin once and for all, it was a free-for-all. Now, here's the good news — when sin wants to destroy our lives, we take it to the Cross to kill it. And here's even more good news: He killed it for good!

There was a man in England who put his Rolls-Royce on a ferry boat and went across to the continent to go on a vacation. While he was driving around Europe, something happened to the motor of his car. He called the Rolls-Royce people back in England and said, *"I'm having trouble with my car; what do you suggest I do?"* Immediately, the Rolls-Royce people flew a mechanic over! He was there in 4 hours! The mechanic repaired the car and flew back to England and left the man to continue his vacation.

As you can imagine, the man was wondering, "How much is this going to cost me? They flew a mechanic over to fix it! It's going to cost a fortune!" When he got back to England, he wrote Rolls-Royce a letter inquiring about how much he owed them. He received a letter from the Rolls-Royce office that read: *"Dear Sir: There is no record anywhere in our files that anything ever went wrong with a Rolls-Royce."* Folks, do you get it? That's salvation in Christ. God did it! You can't pay for your sins. You can't wipe them out. You can't escape them on your own… only in Christ can we do it.

> *Satan tells me I am unworthy; but I always was unworthy, and yet You have long loved me; and therefore my unworthiness cannot be a barrier to having fellowship with You now.* -CH Spurgeon

Friends, understand the Cross deals with sin… and it's the Resurrection now that deals with life.

- There is now the ability to Really Live

> *If the Spirit of him who raised Jesus from the dead dwells in you, he who raised Christ Jesus from the dead will also give life to your mortal bodies through his Spirit who dwells in you.* -Romans 8:11

If you are drowning in confusion and depression today, it's the Resurrection that lifts you up! When Christ is in you, and you know the power of the Cross and the Resurrection, you believe the Truth that He and He alone has taken away your sin. Then you see the fruits of forgiveness in this old tired world, and the fruits of servanthood in your own life. And then you know you are a believer and a follower of the King! God knows exactly what is going on this world today and He has you exactly where He wants you today — set to realize that it's all about Him and not you!

> *In heaven, we shall see that we had not one trial too many.*   -CH Spurgeon

Eternity with Christ is so good that you will not remember the trials on earth. There is no way the fantastic images of glory, and the incredible relational experiences with God will be marginalized or diminished by our past problems. Why? It's the reason Jesus came... to destroy sin and to deliver us from its bondage.

In the 300's, seventeen hundred years ago, there were three ministers who would go and visit the blessed Anthony the Great, the Christian monk, every year. Two of them would discuss their thoughts on these verses here in Romans about salvation of their souls and the state of their hearts, but the third always remained silent and did not ask him anything. After many visits through the years Anthony asked, *"You often come here to see me, but you never ask me anything."* The third minister replied, *"It is enough for me to see you, Father."*

In a world today where most want to be heard and offer their efforts to cure and heal this broken society, we want to do and do and do and prove and prove and prove that we are good. We want to prove we are better than this, and that we can have victory and overcome the evils that exist and are evident in this sorry world. We want to bow to more and more idols. We want to do away with the laws, thinking we can live off of this inner love that we believe we all possess. By and large, most people think love exists deep down and we just have to bring it out. But we're wrong folks. Without Christ, we are dead – dead in our sins – wrong.

> *If you see yourself as a little sinner, you will inevitably see Jesus as a little savior.*
> *-Martin Luther*

You see, in the flesh it's impossible to please God. And if God is not pleased in this world, then things aren't getting better for it. What needs to happen is for a nation to bow before the King and to do it regularly. When we do, we don't have to say a thing. It's enough for us, it will be enough for you, to be with Him. It's enough to see Him, and to see Him work and give you His peace. When we do, we will know He is in us.

Chapter Five

It's fun to say it: *Romans 8 is the greatest chapter in the Bible*. It's detailed. It details what it means to live the Christ-filled life. It's assurance and direction on how to follow Christ. But let me tell you something: before you go diving into chapter eight thinking that all of your problems in life are going to be solved once you read it – that you are going to get your Jesus diploma – hold on. It's just the opposite. Getting involved in Romans 8 just enrolls you in the school to knowing Christ, and you have a lifetime of study, assignments, and attendance. You will be in class until Jesus comes for you. Can I stress it enough? Romans 8 is *so good*. We read it and we say repeatedly, "Oh!

Now I get it!" Or, "Okay, that's not what I heard someone say, but this is what God says!"

And today… today! We all get a gift! It is the gift of all gifts, and I know you want to get ahead of me and say, "Pastor Greg, I know! We know that God's gift to us is His Son who came to take all of our sin upon Himself and to die on a tree! We already know that." Yeah, I know you know it, and it is the ultimate gift. But while you are collecting God's blessings and gifts for your life, don't overlook this one. Everyone gets it. Let's look at it:

> *So don't you see that we don't owe this old do-it-yourself life one red cent. There's nothing in it for us, nothing at all. The best thing to do is give it a decent burial and get on with your new life. God's Spirit beckons. There are things to do and places to go! This resurrection life you received from God is not a timid, grave-tending life. It's adventurously expectant, greeting God with a childlike "What's next, Papa?" God's Spirit touches our spirits and confirms who we really are. We know who he is, and we know who we are: Father and children. And we know we are going to get what's coming to us—an unbelievable inheritance! We go through exactly what Christ goes through. If we go*

through the hard times with him, then we're certainly going to go through the good times with him!
                                        -Romans 8:12-17 MSG

Did you see your gift? Did you get it? Have you unwrapped it? It's obvious isn't it? In a world where we fear rejection more than anything, God solves the problem for us. In this sorry society we endure, where loneliness is rampant and where we are refused and refused again. Where we have racial divide because some — some — claim a special freedom or honor or license. God solves everything by giving us, those in Christ, the privilege above all privileges! Maybe you missed it because you tore open the box, and the gift is sort of the wrapping paper. He gives it to everyone here that knows God, in a relationship with Jesus Christ — and *that* is you and me. *We get to call Him "Father"! "Papa."*

Calling Him *Papa* wasn't a foreign thing to the Jews, but it was not normal. God was over there on that mountain to them, and when you visited, every once in a while, you had to stand back. You stood back because that's how God wanted it, and He wanted it that way because of His holiness and our sinfulness.

But Jesus, the Son, arrives and builds a bridge or, in modern terminology, an Interstate to the Father. The Cross of Jesus Christ is the connection. Now every day is the Father's Day and every day you get to live

Father's Day. Every day you get to call Him Papa. Every day... your gift, my gift, our gift, is that we get to call Him that adoring and endearing term, *Dad*. It's an affectionate term, and it's not formal anymore. It is now the ability to ask, to talk, and to communicate with Him because by the term "Father" we know He is really listening, He wants to listen. He desires to listen to you and me. He is also pleased that we come to Him via the Son and that we spend our time with Him. Now look — this is a mighty big gift. This stuff doesn't just happen! It's not like one day the Bible says, *"Ohhhhh, God forgot to tell y'all that you can call Him dad now!"*

There is a catalyst. Something has happened. Yes, Christ is risen. There is the third person of the Trinity that makes application for your life and mine. Paul tells us that we are no longer led around by the flesh. Stop! The Greek word for flesh here is σαρκα (sarka) and it's difficult to interpret. The best or closest two words are "sinful nature." Don't think Paul was talking about the stuff that hangs off of your bones, nor is he referring to a sexual sin. No, he's talking about where we come from. And at this point, you might say, "Why does this matter in a world where we are tearing ourselves apart racially and politically?" It's not learned behavior, and that is massive to our understanding today. Do you get it yet? He means we are all capable of sinning in the worst way. Quit thinking that you have discovered some utopian love down deep when, really, love is alien and God comes to put it in us.

So, what should we do? You and I are to live by the Spirit! Who is He? What does it mean to live by the Spirit? Beware of charlatans! Run from people who think that they have the Holy Spirit completely figured out and who refer to Him exclusively in weird, outlandish, and completely mystical terms. Those people are often too super-spiritual for me. Too many times our jargon defines our relationship to the Spirit instead of our knowledge. He is a mysterious God, but He wants you to *know* Him and the Bible tells us about the Spirit and what He does in Romans 8. Let's look at four things He does, or four characteristics of the Holy Spirit. Why don't we know who He is or give Him the same value we give the Father and the Son, Jesus?

4 Truths of the Holy Spirit

- He is the Spirit of <u>Holiness</u>

> *For if you live according to the flesh you will die, but if <u>by the Spirit</u> you put to death the deeds of the body, you will live.*
> *-Romans 8:13*

"By the Spirit" is a fancy, spiritual thing to say. It sounds like we are important and all spiritual like when we are talking to someone spiritual and we throw in there, *"Well... I was led by the Spirit."* And people jump

back in awe and do a mental clap of applause for your advancement with the most-high God. *"Whoa! Oh! Wow! He is led by the Spirit, he says. He must be super advanced in knowing God."* Listen, God is not impressed with you and me showing off our spiritual prowess. Look at verse 14 again, this time in the ESV:

> *For all who are led by the Spirit of God are sons of God.* -Romans 8:14

Led to what? Paul is not saying or referring to our being led to start an organization to heal the land. He is not saying "God led me to say to you…." No, no, no. Always in interpretation of the Word of God you have to read it in context, context, and context! If we go back to verse 13, we find Paul telling us – begging us – to kill sin in our lives. So, we are being led to what? Led to live a holy life.

Just recently I was listening to a man introduce the church he was starting, and he was outlining the vision and the core values that the church would be following. One of the very first things he talked about was the value of sacrifice to the church. He was of course talking about money! Okay, let's give him the benefit of the doubt and say he was talking about time, or spiritual talents and gifts. It still doesn't make it any better. God is not spellbound by the amounts of cash we flash His way. I was shocked that this would-be pastor didn't mention anything about holy living. To obey is better than sacrifice. To obey is the beginning of a holy life unto the Lord.

Don't wake up tomorrow and say, "I'm going to start living holy." You can't do it. Paul is saying, "You have to be led by the Spirit."

> ...work out your own salvation with fear and trembling, for it is God who works in you, both to will and to work for his good pleasure. -Philippians 2:12-13

Every act we engage in to grow in Christ must be in participation with the Spirit.

- He is the Spirit of <u>Grace</u>

> For you did not receive the <u>spirit of slavery</u> to fall back into fear, but you have received the Spirit of adoption as sons, by whom we cry, "Abba! Father!
> -Romans 8:15

The old Scottish church asked a question when you wanted to join the church, "Have you been to Sinai?" Sinai was the place where Moses encountered the burning bush. It was the place where God said, "Moses take off your shoes, you are on holy ground." It was the place where Moses realized who God is. Have you been to Sinai? Have you felt Sinai's power? Have you realized your sin against a Holy God? Do you realize that when you are in His presence that you are on holy ground?

The problem with the modern-day church is that we have been pushing it as a place where you can be successful and if you join up, then all your problems will be over. I have a term for that: horse…hockey. Sinai is where you know you are a sinner and you need the Holy Spirit. Stop being flippant when you come to God. Now look at verse 15:

> For you did not receive the _spirit of slavery_ to fall back into fear….

Before we have Christ in our lives we live in bondage, and in slavery to sin. So when Christ sets you free, you are truly free. Now when you first come to Christ you may feel a burdensome conviction for your sin, and that you can't please Him. Yes, many feel a spirit of slavery. Listen to me, this is massive, and I mean very massive to us and will catapult you into a major step of spiritual growth: We may very well feel defeated and depressed in this world today… we may feel without hope even as a Christian, but He leads you to freedom and He frees you!

Remember the story Jesus tells about the Prodigal Son? The Father throws a huge party of celebration and kills the fatted calf. That's veal chops, veal scallopine, braised veal… And remember the older brother and how mad and incensed he gets? "What do you mean throwing a party for that scoundrel? He took your money! He wasted it all! And you throw a party for him? What's the deal?" Do you remember what the older brother said? "All these years I've *slaved* for you." And the father responded, "But you've always been my son."

You see the older brother's perception of his dad was one of slavery. It was one where he thought his dad loved the other son better than him. The older brother believed his dad was giving to that prodigal boy more than he was giving to him.

We, as Christians, erroneously believe the same thing too often. We believe God loves other Christians more than us. "He must!" we say… "Look at all they have!" Don't you feel that sometimes? You pick a flower and pull off the petals, "He loves me, He loves me not…." We have this kind of insecurity about our relationship with God.

Paul is saying God brings you out of slavery and sets you free! Look at the second part:

> …but you have received <u>the Spirit of adoption as sons,</u> by whom we cry, "Abba! Father!"   -Romans 8:15b

In the old city, Jerusalem, a Hasidic Jew was running, he was late for Sabbath worship, and he had in tow his four-year-old boy, holding onto his hand.

And you could hear the tap, tap, tap of the Jewish dad's shoes running. And the little boy, barely hitting the ground every four or five steps, was saying, "Abba, Abba, Abba, Abba…." It was a cry out to his dad. Abba, God is our Father. We too, are in grace and can cry out to God our dad.

- He is the Spirit of <u>Adoption</u>

> …but you have received <u>the Spirit of</u> <u>adoption as sons</u>, by whom we cry, "Abba! Father!"   -Romans 8:15b

Paul is not interested in being politically correct. When he uses the word "sons" you can't add daughters here because the Romans wouldn't have a clue what you were talking about. It would make no sense for him to say sons and daughters but of course that's what he means. Besides the highlight is not political correctness, it's the adoption.

Jesus taught us to pray, "Our Father, who art in heaven…." I know that some have had tumultuous relationships with your dads, and some have had absentee dads. So, in this case, instead of comparison to find an understanding, you have to contrast that type of dad. The Scriptures say we get to call Him Abba… Father… it's that sweet a term of affection. It can be akin to that feeling you get every year on Father's Day when you think about your dad and want to spend time with him, or the dad who may be gone and you think about those special times. It's that feeling multiplied and forever-lasting for those adopted in Christ. We've gained so much in the Gospel, we are a family! We are children in a family! And He is our Father.

The other night Jack, my son, texted me and said, "Dad, I need to ask you are question... can I call you in an hour?" It was around 8pm. I texted him back, "Of course." Jack was being respectful, but I want him to know that if it was 3:00 a.m. and he texted and said, "Can I call?" I would say, "Of course!" If he called and said, "Dad, can you fly up tomorrow and see me?" The answer would be "Of course!" If he needed money, or anything in the world for that matter, the answer from me is going to be "Of course," because he is my son.

When we are adopted by God we didn't grow up in the family, but He brings us in, signs the papers, and justifies us. The Psalms say He forever forgets about the sin. Scripture tells us even the blood of the Savior is over me, is over you, if you are Christ.

What makes the New Testament new? One of the significant ways is the doctrine of adoption. You see, in the Old Testament it was rare that God was mentioned as Father. He was there, not here. The name was Yahweh, or Jehovah, and they drove the memory of the way they even spelled it out of their minds. Even today, Jewish scholars disagree with how even to pronounce it. His name was so holy, they wouldn't even say it! But now — now, Paul says, we get to call Him Abba… Father.

- He is the Spirit of <u>Witness</u>

> *…by whom we cry, "Abba! Father!" The Spirit himself bears witness with our spirit that we are children of God….*
> *-Romans 8:15b, 16*

Cry is an important word here. It's the same word for cry that we find when Jesus cried in the Garden before He went to the Cross. It means pain, it means derelict. We can go to Him when things are not good and call Him Father. He gave His Son, and He knows. He knows the pain of that suffering childhood you had that haunts you today. He knows the pain of just being diagnosed. He knows the suffering of those in a marriage on its last leg. He knows. We get to cry out to Him.

When Adam and Eve were in the Garden, the snake came to Eve, "Hey, didn't God tell you not to touch the tree?" And Eve said, "Why, yes… I believe He did." When He didn't actually say that at all. He said, "Don't eat from the tree." Maybe that means you can climb the tree, hang a hammock in the tree, build a treehouse, and even drill a hole in the tree. Maybe even cut off a few limbs to burn. But God said, "Don't eat from it." As Eve pondered the question for a moment she is thinking, "Maybe He doesn't love us as much as we thought." Oh, the power of suggestion from the enemy.

The Holy Spirit is a witness to the love of God. When we are about to throw in the towel, begin question and doubt, and forget God, the Holy Spirit reminds us and witnesses to us that He loves us.

I read this recently:

Let me know if God has rejected you. Let the church and the pastor know if God has said "no" to you… because if He has, then you are the very first one in the history of the world!

Who is He, the Holy Spirit? He leads us to holiness. He tells us of God's grace that sets us free. He shows us how we are adopted. He is a witness to and for God, the Father.

I've said a lot today, now let me sum it up for you in a text message:

- # Religion: I messed up! My dad is going to kill me.

- # Christian: I messed up! I need to call my dad.

Chapter Six

Here are some recent headlines:

- Apocalyptic virus surges feared in major US cities
- Angry residents erupt at meeting over new mask rule
- Dr. Gupta says time is running out for America
- Chicago girl, 13, was dancing with mom when she was killed by stray bullet in home
- Miley Cyrus talks about sobriety
- White Jesus statues should be torn down

Death, disease, and disaster are commonplace in our world, and they have been for thousands of years. We've just chosen to ignore God in them. Just this week I heard someone say, *"I'm not just looking for Jesus to return anymore, I'm listening for the trumpet."* We are in this fantastic – I mean stupendous – study in the book of Romans. I call Romans 8 *the greatest chapter in the Bible*. Why? It's pure, beautiful theology... not that the rest of the Bible isn't... but this is Paul's precise, succinct presentation of life and how to live it. Let's look at today's passage:

> *For I consider that the sufferings of this present time are not worth comparing with the glory that is to be revealed to us. For the creation waits with eager longing for the revealing of the sons of God. For the creation was subjected to futility, not willingly....*   *-Romans 8:18-25*

- There's no comparison of this day & that day to come

Have you heard about Chippie the parakeet? He never saw it coming. One second he was peacefully perched in his cage. The next he was sucked in, washed up, and blown over. The problems began when Chippie's owner decided to clean his cage with a vacuum cleaner. She removed the attachment from the end of the hose and stuck it in the cage. The phone rang, and she turned to pick it up. She'd barely said "hello" when "ssssopp!" Chippie got sucked in.

The bird owner gasped, put down the phone, turned off the vacuum, and opened the bag. There was Chippie — still alive, but stunned. Since the bird was covered with dust and soot, she grabbed him and raced to the bathroom, turned on the faucet, and held Chippie under the running water. Then, realizing that Chippie was soaked and shivering, she did what any compassionate bird owner would do… she reached for the hair dryer and blasted the pet with hot air. Poor Chippie never knew what hit him.

A few days after the trauma, the reporter who'd initially written about the event contacted Chippie's owner to see how the bird was recovering. "Well," she replied, "Chippie doesn't sing much anymore — he just sits and stares."

It's easy to see why. Sucked in, washed up, and blown over…. That's enough to steal the song from the healthiest of hearts. It's wild, it's the same thing that's happened to the American church! We've been sucked in, and many are washed up and have been blown over! It's time to get back to trusting God, whatever the circumstances!

Creation is longing for redemption, and Creation is subject to futility. Creation is in bondage to decay, yet Creation is in birth pangs. Paul starts out with "For I consider…." In the King James Version, it's *"For I reckon."* Reckon means to count. When Paul makes the comparison of suffering versus what is to come, there is no comparison. There's no comparison to the strife, pain, hurt, tension, wounds, bleeding, disease, and bullets of today compared to being with Him. When you look at glory, when you look forward to heaven, when you contemplate no more sin, no more tears, no more hurt… you can't come close to saying, "Well, being with God is just not worth it." David, in writing the twenty-seventh Psalm says,

> *One thing have I asked of the Lord,*
>   *that will I seek after:*
> *that I may dwell in the house of the Lord*
>   *all the days of my life,*
> *to gaze upon the beauty of the Lord*
>   *and to inquire in his temple.*
>   *-Psalm 27:4*

There's no comparison! Often overlooked when we look at the Crucifixion, and the Resurrection… is the Ascension. Jesus ascended to the right hand of the Father, to be with Him in glory. Folks, glory is where those who are in Christ will dwell eternally.

I believe the enemy, Satan, has rows and rows of attacks planned lined up for us. He's laying traps for this world. I believe he is conniving and insidious, plotting to fool us into thinking that we can outrun our sin or that God is going to give us a pass at the last second.

I see the racial divide. I hear about the Coronavirus. I feel the uneasiness of social distancing. Our country is split in two politically. We were told of killer bees coming a few weeks ago… and according to the State paper the other day, great whites have made the South Carolina coast their feeding ground for the summer. What's next? It used to be we wanted out of 2020, but no one dares peek into 2021! I believe Satan uses all of this this to throw us off the prize of glory. The enemy wants to distract you and me, and for us to make the statement under our breath, "I just don't know if all this is worth it." With that in mind, read Scripture and you will find that all the writers are writing guided by the hand of God to remind us, enlighten us, to His glory and how wonderful it is.

Look at this Scripture in the Message translation:

That's why I don't think there's any comparison between the present hard times and the coming good times. The created world itself can hardly wait for what's coming next. Everything in creation is being more or less held back. God reins it in until both creation and all the creatures are ready and can be released at the same moment into the glorious times ahead. Meanwhile, the joyful anticipation deepens.

All around us we observe a pregnant creation. The difficult times of pain throughout the world are simply birth pangs. But it's not only around us; it's within us. The Spirit of God is arousing us within. We're also feeling the birth pangs. These sterile and barren bodies of ours are yearning for full deliverance. That is why waiting does not diminish us, any more than waiting diminishes a pregnant mother. We are enlarged in the waiting. We, of course, don't see what is enlarging us. But the longer we wait, the larger we become, and the more joyful our expectancy. -Romans 8:18-25 MSG

- Be anxious for "nothing," Be patient for "everything"

Most have been looking at it the wrong way. It's not that the world is about to end, no… not at all. That's a demonic way of looking at things. Ending? The enemy wants to end it for you. The enemy's vocabulary is to end your happiness, to end your livelihood, to end your passion for God, and to end your life. He wants to end this world, and he wants to end *your* world. He wants to end the things of God, he wants to end prosperity, and he wants to end the church. What is Paul saying to us? It's not the ending of this world, but it's the beginning of the transition to God's beautiful creation.

We live in a fallen world – one that without God is meaningless. Paul says, "futility." Futile means *ineffective*. In the end, it means nothing. Will you have spent all these years in your life working, toiling, saving, spending, gobbling up, taking, stealing, accumulating, amassing, and hoarding? If you do, then you will get to the end and you will find out that you really can't take it with you. You will learn the hard way that they really haven't found a way to freeze your head and bring you back with a new body five hundred years from now. Futility is synonymous with that word that's used in the book of Ecclesiastes:

> *Vanity of vanities, says the Preacher, vanity of vanities! All is vanity. What does man gain by all the toil at which he toils under the sun? A generation goes, and a generation comes, but the earth remains forever. The sun rises, and the sun goes down, and hastens to the place where it rises.* -Ecclesiastes 1:1-5

The word *vanity* in Ecclesiastes is the word that's *futility* here in Romans 8. What's life worth living for? It's futile without God. But with God, it's everything! What we are discovering here, in Romans 8, is that Paul… listen, this is where the rubber meets the road for us… is saying we are sitting in two zip codes.

Paul tells us back in verse 17, that we are heirs. We have eternal life because of what Jesus did on the Cross. He died for us. Remember in part five where it says we have been adopted, we are heirs, fellow heirs with Christ? Jesus is with the Father in His Kingdom. We too, those in Christ, will be in that Kingdom. Our souls have been redeemed but in this body we suffer, he says. Some Christians suffer more than others, but everybody suffers. And sometimes we suffer for the sins of others. We didn't do it, but we suffer anyway.

Job suffered. He lost ten children. He lost his 401k. He lost his health. He lost the respect of his wife. And it wasn't because of sin in his life. Job was a right-living guy. Life is like that. We suffer. Job's friends, however, wanted to blame him, thinking it was some sin in Job's life that they didn't know about. And that is the name of the tune that they kept harping on and singing for the entire book! Understand this — this will help you understand this crazy, wild world of pain. Whatever it is — family, relationships, job, money, race, disease, health —here it is:

- We live in the tension of the <u>Now</u> & <u>Not Yet</u>

We are children of God, but we are not as we should be yet.

...we are God's children now, and what we will be has not yet appeared; but we know that when he appears we shall be like him, because we shall see him as he is.   *-1 John 3:2*

We live in the *now* and *not yet* but there is a part of the not yet that has broken into the now. The eternal Christ arrived. He overcame the grave and rose from the dead so that you too could have life eternal in a Resurrected body. Last chapter we talked about the Holy Spirit. He applies salvation to you and me. There is now regeneration, life assurance, and we can call Him "Abba, Father"! The *not yet* has broken into the now. But we are still here... there is decay, futility, and birth pangs.

For eight months we waited. It's usually nine, I know, but the birth pangs for my wife were increasing. The signs of our son's arrival were upon us. She was admitted to the hospital and the nurse came in and said, "Just get comfortable, it will be a while." And I said, "Do I have time to go to the bathroom?" It was 5:45 in the afternoon, and she said, "Honey, take your time, this baby isn't going to arrive until after midnight! I walked down the hall to the bathroom and was washing my hands when my mother-in-law came in the door yelling, "C'mon, the baby is coming!" It had only been five minutes! I rushed in, Missie is in labor, the doctor is there, the nurse said, "Put on a gown, put on a gown!" And the doctor said, there is no time… just let him be without one! It was a rush! Jack was in a rush. The doctors were in a rush. Missie was in birth pangs.

What does Paul mean by birth pangs? He means God is going to restore things, and we are waiting for Him to do so, and it hurts to live in this world, but heaven is coming! God is working His plan for our lives daily. Isaiah talks about it in chapters 65 and 66. There's going to be a new heaven and new earth. It is what Peter talks about:

> *But do not overlook this one fact, beloved, that with the Lord one day is as a thousand years, and a thousand years as one day. The Lord is not slow to fulfill his promise as some count slowness, but is patient toward you, not wishing that any should perish, but that all should reach repentance. <u>But the day of the Lord will come like a thief, and then the heavens will pass away with a roar</u>, and the heavenly bodies will be burned up and dissolved, and the earth and the works that are done on it will be exposed.*
> *-2 Peter 3:8-10*

There is going to be liberation from futility.

For in him all the fullness of God was pleased to dwell, and through him to reconcile to himself all things, whether on earth or in heaven, making peace by the blood of his cross.   -Colossians 1:19,20

Repent therefore, and turn back, that your sins may be blotted out, that times of refreshing may come from the presence of the Lord, and that he may send the Christ appointed for you, Jesus, whom heaven must receive until the time for restoring all the things about which God spoke by the mouth of his holy prophets long ago.   -Acts 3:19-21

Jesus said to them, "Truly, I say to you, in the new world, when the Son of Man will sit on his glorious throne....
-Matthew 19:28

Creation is going to be born again. Don't you see that the Holy Spirit is the guarantee of the Harvest that is to come? The birth pangs hurt! Oh, it hurts. But there is a day coming when we will no longer struggle with sin and the ramifications of it.

Life at this point, in the summer of 2020, stinks doesn't it? You may use another word to describe it, but it's a mess. Things that have been said, things that have been done, and are beyond solvable. The strange, strange thing in this modern-day culture: we look everywhere for the answer, yet the one place we mock is the place where the answer is found.

We think the answer is in politics. We think it's in peace that the hippies describe. We think it's in money or Wall Street. We think it's in jobs. We think it's in art. We think it's about sports. We think it's about a vaccine. We think it's about the right Supreme Court. And now, we think that the only way forward is to totally forget the past. None of those things come even close to solving it.

> *For in this hope we were saved. Now hope that is seen is not hope.*
> *-Romans 8:24*

Hope here is not a wishful hope, but a guarantee. I guarantee it. I guarantee He is coming again soon. And let me tell you what else is coming soon: more hard times for the church, suffering for the Christian, the end of American society as we know it, of childhood, of teenage life, of young adulthood. These things, in the ways we have become accustomed to them, are all coming to an end. That is why we have this hope in Christ that is *firm and secure like an anchor*, as the Hebrews writer tells us. There is suffering here, but glory to come.

But, as it is written,   "What   no   eye has seen, nor ear heard, nor the heart of man imagined, what God has prepared for those who love him."

-1 Corinthians 2:9

You can't just imagine heaven. You can't dream up in your mind, or I in mine, what His glory is all about. You can't picture it! Isaiah was blown away by it in Isaiah chapter one. John was amazed and staggering from what he saw in the Revelation. Listen, it's worth it! Let me tell you, in case no has before: in your suffering and in your pain and in your hurt, He is worth it! In your tears and crying and tortuous days, He is worth it! In your disillusionment, your worry, and your confusion about these days... He is worth it! Folks, when this sorry world drives you into the dust and dirt of life, worship Him there! He's worth it!

Chapter Seven

It's pretty easy for me to think about keeping the Ten Commandments... in practice. I mean, I woke up this morning and I didn't say, *"Today, I'm going out and I'm going to steal something!"* I know it's wrong, and I know what's right when it comes to personal property. I am not going to spend the week cussing God and taking His name in vain. I am also not going out and carving a piece of wood into a god, put it on my dresser and worship to it every day. It's not me, it never has been, and I can state confidently that I will never do it. One of my favorite authors and theologians and preachers, A.W. Pink, said, *"If you complain about the rain, then really, you are complaining about God."* It has a lot of truth to it. I may not act against God, but let me tell you, I complain a lot about what He does even if it is just to myself.

I am like many of you. I am disciplined in my giving, regular in my serving, and upfront and honest with God and others. I don't make up any excuses when it comes to giving because there "ain't" none. I pretty much do unto others as I want done unto me, even though what's done to me many times is *not* how I did others. As far as I know, next week I'll be in church – and the week after that, and the week after that, and the following week. I know me, I will be in church. I know me, I will sing during the worship time. I know me, I will listen to the sermon, the lesson, or the Bible Study. I know me, I will support mission causes. I know me, I will comply and wear a mask. I know me, I will complain about the COVID details, but I will tip good when I go out. I know me. I know I will do some good stuff. And when it comes down to the most important thing you can exercise on this planet, the most important thing you can do, the best thing you can do, the hardest thing to do… I know me, and I will hem and haw and make excuses and even justify it and say I don't have time… I know me, and when it comes to praying… let's just say I will make excuses to God. When it comes to praying, I have come to study it, participate in it, do it, get pretty good at it, I guess. But I don't get it or understand it all the time. It's still the most difficult thing I do. It's elusive for me, if that makes any sense. Prayer is an enigma for me. But one thing I do, I keep seeking Him in prayer and studying prayer and participating in prayer. And you should be also!

Romans 8 has everything — everything that is important to you and me for understanding the Christian life. And today's message in Romans 8:26,27 is that message that you have been looking for. It's the secret of prayer. Yes, it seems there has been a secret all these years that many of us didn't realize. So secret, that many have missed it. I want someone to come up to me afterwards and say, "Where has this message been? Why hasn't the church let me in on this important truth?" Just two verses to look at in this chapter from Romans 8:

> Likewise _the Spirit helps us in our weakness_. For **we do not know what to pray for** as we ought, but the _Spirit himself intercedes for us_ with groanings too deep for words. And he who searches hearts _knows what is the mind of the Spirit_, because the Spirit intercedes for the saints according to the will of God.
> -Romans 8:26,27

- There is struggle in prayer

I struggle in prayer... you do too. We are weak in prayer. Some are strong in spiritual gifts, some are strong in attendance, some are strong inviting people to church, and some are strong in giving. But many, many have a weakness in prayer. Everyone struggles in prayer. Why? Because it doesn't work! Say it again?! Prayer doesn't work... not the way most people understand it. Do you mean to tell me that it is profitable for me, it is commanded of me, it behooves me, it pleases God when I do it, it is the only way to truly live by faith, and without it I am not really a God-fearer, Christ-follower? You mean to tell me that one of the greatest acts I can participate in on the face of the planet today to further the Kingdom of Almighty God, to relieve the earth of the cycle of pain, to come to the rescue of thousands and thousands and millions and millions... you mean to tell me that the absolute greatest act I can be involved in today on a spiritual level, a physical level, and even emotionally is to get on my knees, bow my head, close my eyes and talk out loud to someone I can't see, whom I really don't hear back from Him with these ears in an audible way like I am hearing you... you mean to tell me that even if I don't talk out loud to Him, *He still hears me*? You mean to tell me... what you are saying is that more than the millions of dollars we can give to cure world hunger, more than all the vaccines we can invent to cure disease, more than all the relief we can give to the down-and-out, more than all the shelter we can give to those living on the street, more than concrete answers to life's real problems... you mean to tell me that the best thing I can ever do is to pray? To ask the ceiling, ask the wall, turn out the lights by closing my eyes, act like someone is there? What kind of nonsense is this?

Don't you see why prayer doesn't work? It's because we really don't engage in the prayer that the Word of God is calling us to! Prayer is another one of those Christian acts that has to be led by faith. He's there. If you are not struggling in prayer, if you are not wanting to resist it, to fight it, then I would wonder if you are growing in Christ.

o Part of the struggle is whether or not you believe in it…
o Part of the weakness is our doubt
o Part of the struggle is whether or not you engage in it…
o Part of the weakness is we don't really know God
o Part of the struggle is wrestling with having time to pray…
o Part of the weakness is our lack of trust
o Part of the struggle is whether or not you care about life…
o Part of the weakness… we don't get down on our knees and look up with our eyes
o Part of the struggle… whether or not you believe in the One you are praying to…

Serving at church, attending church, going to church, attending online, going on mission work trips, reading my Bible, giving, giving until it hurts, all these things I can get involved in with little to no effort or question... but prayer? It sounds so good to say it, but where are the prayer police? Who is checking up on you? I joke when I see on Facebook someone cry out and say, "Where are my prayer warriors?" and "Calling all prayer warriors!" It's like the Superfriends or Marvel Superheroes. I'll be honest, I've read about prayer warriors...I've known a couple... a couple, but not many. George Mueller was a prayer warrior, and so was Mr. Rees Howells, but candidly, I don't know men like that today.

Let me be more honest with you. If you would ask me the greatest need in our church right now, it's not a student minister, it's not three million dollars to build what we want to build, it's not space, it's not another guitarist, it's not more perfect Christians, it's not Billy Graham, it's not the Apostle Paul personally sitting down with you and answering some questions on the Christian life. It's prayer. It's a few men and women who will commit themselves to getting alone – going into a closet, out in the woods, sitting in your car – and crying out to God... asking God for help.

Job struggled in life after he lost everything to no fault of his own. He didn't do anything wrong! Yet he struggled and wrestled with God, asking why? Why? Why? And when Satan is allowed to take away Job's stuff, he was lonely. Loneliness is a killer. Loneliness in life is a prayer killer. If the enemy can get you to stop praying by filling your life with other stuff, then it cuts off your lifeline to God. And when that happens you want to die in misery, because without God you are indeed lonely. Job shows us that when you get to the point of misery in your life, you will even give up God. I see it happen all the time.

Elijah struggled and wanted to give up when he was obedient to God, yet Jezebel wanted to kill him. This over-burdensome life will kill you or make you wish you were dead. And when you get away from the interaction with God in prayer, there's no telling where your mind spins off to.

> *When Elijah saw how things were, he ran for dear life to Beersheba, far in the south of Judah. He left his young servant there and then went on into the desert another day's journey. He came to a lone broom bush and collapsed in its shade, wanting in the worst way to be done with it all—to just die: "Enough of this, God! Take my life—I'm ready to join my ancestors in the grave!* -1 Kings 19:3,4 MSG

Life was a struggle and talking to God was a struggle for Elijah. The Apostle Paul is struggling in 2

Corinthians 12. We don't know what it is about for sure, but most think it's his eyesight:

> *...so I wouldn't get a big head, I was given the gift of a handicap to keep me in constant touch with my limitations. Satan's angel did his best to get me down; what he in fact did was push me to my knees. No danger then of walking around high and mighty! At first I didn't think of it as a gift, and begged God to remove it. Three times I did that, and then he told me, 'My grace is enough; it's all you need. My strength comes into its own in your weakness.'*
>
> *-2 Corinthians 12:7,8 MSG*

Here's what we learn from Paul's struggles: When God says I gave it to you — When God says, I caused it so that you would seek Me more — is that answer good enough for you? Prayer is a struggle, we struggle in it because we are weak, and in it we see not our every wish granted, but God's will and measure and plan done in our lives for His glory!

Jesus struggled in prayer. He was in the Garden, the Cross was looming large as the night crept on. The soldiers were getting close to arrest Him, His disciples who were told to stay in that one place and do that one thing — pray — couldn't do it. They struggled like we struggle sometimes to stay awake. What were they supposed to do? Wash your face!

> *Watch and pray that you may not enter into temptation. The spirit indeed is willing, but the flesh is weak.*
> *-Matthew 26:41*

Jesus, in His human side, knew what was coming. The cross wasn't some new form of death penalty created for Jesus. Everyone knew the pain and agony of hanging on a cross until you died. Everyone was familiar with it, even if they refused to attend. They had heard the stories, they knew it wasn't just a death sentence, but it was to make a point, to make you suffer as long as possible and then die. In other words, folks, it was going to hurt. The emotional struggle leading up to the time was enough. Think about everyone that needed attention every day with a touch of the Lord, healing, a word, a sermon, a rescue, all while you have to carry around the burden that in a few weeks, a few days, they are going to nail you up on that tree, and the blood is going to drip off your mangled body. And the ones that are going to put you there are, even now, the ones that you are helping!

> *Leaving there, he went, as he so often did, to Mount Olives. The disciples followed him. When they arrived at the place, he*

said, "Pray that you don't give in to temptation."

He pulled away from them about a stone's throw, knelt down, and prayed, "Father, remove this cup from me. But please, not what I want. What do you want?" At once an angel from heaven was at his side, strengthening him. He prayed on all the harder. Sweat, wrung from him like drops of blood, poured off his face.

He got up from prayer, went back to the disciples and found them asleep, drugged by grief. He said, "What business do you have sleeping? Get up. Pray so you won't give in to temptation." No sooner were the words out of his mouth than a crowd showed up, Judas, the one….   *-Luke 22:39-47*

Why is praying a struggle? Because it is struggling with the providence of God. It's a struggle because it teaches us and leads us to give up our way and give ourselves over to Him and His best for our lives.

- You desperately need help in prayer

*…but the <u>Spirit himself intercedes for us</u>
with groanings too deep for words. - v.26*

This is the last thing we learn about what the Holy Spirit does in Romans 8. Remember the other things? Let me tell you: many, many go crazy with trying to grasp the Holy Spirit and who He is and what He does. He is part of the Trinity. Our God is one, in three persons. He is not, he is *not*, one entity manifesting Himself in different ways. He is ONE. He is the Spirit of Holiness. He points us and leads us to righteous living – right living. That's primary! He is the Spirit of Grace. He shows us God's grace. It's His forgiveness and love. He shows us how, in Christ, we have been adopted by God. We are born into sin, we are born again, from above, and grafted into Christ. He is also a witness – bears witness to God and to the Son. And here He intercedes for us. We have another who intercedes for us, too. Yes, we have two! Jesus intercedes for us.

What is the deal here? Not only is it a struggle, but we don't know what to pray. We're so burdened about our world – about our government, about our outlook, about the election, about COVID, about other potential viruses out there, about the fall and life with some semblance of normal – that we are overwhelmed. We have no clue what the answer is. Then, we will give up easily. Like Elijah, we don't know! Like Job, we are beaten down. Like Paul, why can't it just be smooth sailing? I would be all right if I was well or rich or lived there or worked there or had this... I need help. Here's why:

> The first great characteristic of us as Christian people, is that we are no longer self-confident. We know the truth about ourselves.   -Martin Lloyd-Jones

We know the truth about ourselves. We don't know how to pray! It's not your confidence, it's humility and lowliness that speak to a great God. We need help. The Holy Spirit, the very definition given to us by the Lord Himself when He was about to leave...

> But the Helper, the Holy Spirit, whom the Father will send in my name, he will teach you all things and bring to your remembrance all that I have said to you.
>   -John 14:26

Jesus doesn't say, "I'm going to send the Holy Spirit so that you can do a bunch of cool miracles to impress your friends, and to tell you exactly what is going on in the world and why God is doing it, so that you will have the inside scoop." Where do we get off thinking the Holy Spirit is our flunky? We need help. The coolest thing in the world is to look back and ponder the fact that the disciples walked with Jesus every day! Go back to the Garden of Eden and the highlight of life was when God visited, and Adam walked with God every day! Don't we see? It's about being with Him every day! The helper helps us do that and understand that.

- To pray is to be successful

When you feel yourself to be utterly unworthy, you have hit the truth.
                              -CH Spurgeon

Listen: behind every great ministry and church, behind every great pastor and leader, behind every incredible missionary, behind the true saints of God that want to make a difference in this world for the glory of God, there is true prayer. Behind every great movement of God, behind every single revival on this planet, there has to be honest, weak in humility, repentance in, and looking up to God, prayer. It was John Wesley who said, "God does nothing except in answer to prayer."

Prayer is success not because we do it, Paul is telling us in Romans 8, but that even when it comes to prayer God chose us, God elected us, God saved us. It was all God's initiative and God's plan and you don't think that He is going to leave the fate of the world to us, do you? Are you joking me? He Himself does it. He sends the Helper and when the Helper is involved in its success, you had better believe it!

When Hudson Taylor was sailing to China to begin his missionary work, his ship was in great danger. Back in the 1840's it took three months to sail to China from Europe. The wind had died, and the current was carrying them toward sunken reefs which were close to islands inhabited by cannibals — so close they could see the cannibals building fires on the shore. They tried everything, but nothing worked. In his journal Taylor recorded what happened next:

> *The Captain said to me, "Well, we have done everything that can be done." A thought occurred to me, and I replied, "No, there is one thing we have not done yet." "What is that?" he queried. "Four of us on board are Christians. Let us each retire to his own cabin, and in agreed prayer ask the Lord to give us immediately a breeze."*

Taylor prayed briefly and then, certain that the answer was coming, went up on the deck and asked the first officer to let down the sails.

> *"What would be the good of that?" he answered roughly. I told him we had been asking a wind from God; that it was coming immediately.*

Within minutes the wind did began to blow, and it carried them safely past the reefs. Taylor wrote:

> *Thus God encouraged me before landing on China's shores to bring every variety of need to Him in prayer, and to expect that He would honour the name of the Lord Jesus and give the help each emergency required.*

Do you know how long it took me to find that story on answered prayer? About five seconds. Google "answered prayer" and you are inundated with stories. Ask your Christian friends about answered prayer and they will have a story, I guarantee. Everywhere, all over this world, there are stories of answered prayer. The impossible stuff that's getting you down and keeping you from going on with God is put there to prove God in your life. Commit your life to prayer and you will see it change. Give yourself to humility and weakness before Him, and He will make you strong in faith. After all, He has given you the Helper to make sense to the Father even though we groan and don't know how to pray. The Holy Spirit goes to God for us.

Chapter Eight

It's 420 A.D., and the barbarians have just invaded Rome. The Roman Empire is on its heels. The entire civilized world was collapsing… falling apart. If you had been alive at this time, everything that you had ever known was being turned upside down. You would self-quarantine because you were scared to death. The fall of Rome was going to eventually lead to the Dark Ages, 500 to 1500. It was a long period of horrible, atrocious times. But – in 420 A.D. there were two Church Fathers, preachers, who were very influential. One was Jerome. He's the guy who had written the Latin Vulgate version of the Bible, which is very important to the translations we have today. The other preacher was Augustine.

As the Barbarians stormed Rome, Jerome, so distraught, so upset, so beside himself, he went into isolation in a cave. He self-quarantined. And he basically died of depression. Because society, civilization, and culture as he knew it, was essentially over. He fell into a deep depression and despair, and he gave up.

The other preacher/bishop, Augustine, wrote a little book, 900+ pages, called *City of God*. In it he takes an entirely different perspective than Jerome. Augustine says,

> *There is the City of Man, which is shifting and changing all throughout human history. Empires rise and fall, economies grow large and robust, and then collapse; time marches on, but the City of God endures forever. It is eternal, and it's the goal of every believer.*

Augustine went on to live for 10 more years, before dying at the age of 75. He went on teaching, preaching, evangelizing, writing books, and making a difference for the Kingdom of God here on earth.

The difference between Jerome and Augustine was their perspective, and their view of God, His sovereignty and His goodness. And the main difference between the two men was where they had placed their hope. One was thinking too much of this earth as home, and the other knew his home was in heaven with the Lord.

Hit the speed button forward to the 1500's. It's the Bubonic Plague. It's spreading like wildfire across Europe. Before it was finished, it would end up killing close to sixty million people and wiping out nearly two-thirds of Europe's population. Around 1527 it spread to Germany. People panicked. People fled. Hysteria, fear, panic, concern — it was all very real during this time. And, let's be honest, it was justified. Sixty million were dead and no cure in sight. If you caught the Black Plague, you were a goner within a week or two. No hope. There was chaos as they ran en masse, like a stampede. The Plague reached Germany and it was like the running of the bulls in Spain. They did not know where they were going or how they would survive away from their farms, jobs, and livelihoods. They just ran.

The great Protestant Reformer Martin Luther and his wife Katherine decided, after spending a lot of time in prayer, that they would stay. And they decided to stay because they saw a huge opportunity for ministry, and service for Christ. They turned their home into a hospital and began ministering to shut-ins and others affected by the Plague. They stayed home so that they could minister to the dying about going home. It was during that time that Luther wrote the hymn "A Mighty Fortress is Our God:"

A mighty Fortress is our God,
a Bulwark never failing.
Our Helper He amid the flood,
of mortal ills prevailing...

Speed up again and jump to 1918. The Spanish Flu is killing people! More than fifty million people worldwide... more than 600,000 here in America. Here are some of the newspaper headlines from that time:

- **The Seattle Daily Times:** Churches, Schools, Shows Closed: Epidemic puts ban on all public assemblies
- **Duluth Herald (Minnesota):** Public Gatherings in Duluth are Forbidden
- **Tacoma Daily Ledger:** City puts ban on funerals in churches; 15 More die of Spanish Influenza
- **San Francisco Chronicle:** Influenza masks play big part in curbing epidemic
- **The Arizona Republican:** Begin Manana everyone must wear flu mask
- **Birmingham News:** Churchless day is planned here: Epidemic of influenza causes ban on all houses of worship

In all of these times – in every instance where we are threatened, stressed, and in pain – we are looking for somewhere to go. We are looking for a fortress. We are looking for a place to hide behind walls. We are looking for that safe place, that safe feel, that safe zone. Many are looking for home.

William J. Kirkpatrick began his songwriting ministry when he was a fife major to the 91st Regiment of the Union army during the Civil War. His wife died in 1878 and he devoted himself to writing hymns. If you grew up in church, perhaps you know them: "Jesus Saves, ""'Tis Sweet to Trust in Jesus," "Redeemed, How I Love to Proclaim It," and "He Hideth My Soul." Kirkpatrick's most famous hymn was written to express his desire to see people come to Jesus and be changed by the power of Christ.

In his later years, he became a much-requested song leader at camp meetings. At one of the meetings, a soloist had been hired to provide the special music. He had a magnificent voice and was able to put tremendous expression into the music he sang. However, William noticed that the young man always left after he finished singing, and never stayed to hear the sermon. Afraid that the soloist was not a Christian, Kirkpatrick knelt in his tent and prayed long and earnestly for the young man's soul. As he prayed, some words began to form in his mind. He wrote them down and set them to a haunting tune.

That evening, William handed the newly-written words and tune to the soloist. Visibly moved after he had sung them, the man stayed for the sermon, went to the altar that night and gave his heart to Christ. The song became a popular invitation hymn in evangelical services, winning many others besides the man it was written for. It was these words, written by William J. Kirkpatrick, that the Holy Spirit used to bring salvation to a lost soul:

> *I've wandered far away from God*
> *Now, I'm coming home*
> *The paths of sin too long I've trod*
> *Lord, I'm coming home.*
> *Coming home, coming home*
> *Never more to roam*
> *Open wide thine arms of love,*
> *Lord, I'm coming home.*

In the spiritual life – the Christian spiritual life – we read God's Word to read His promises. Where are the greatest promises? What is the greatest promise?

Romans 8:28 is that place we begin to look. If you live at the address of 8:28, then your life is stable in turbulent times. If you live within these walls at 8:28 Romans – within this safety, within this fortress and kingdom – then you have a great grip on life and nothing, absolutely nothing can blow you over. 8:28 is a home address… is it yours? No life hurricanes, no enemy tornadoes, and no political winds will harm you. Here it is. It's the great verse in the greatest chapter. Some say the greatest verse in all of the Bible:

And we know that for those who love God all things work together for good, for those who are called according to his purpose.   *-Romans 8:28*

But for those who live outside these walls, outside of 8:28, there is confusion, anxiety, fear, and uncertainty. Outside of this future grace of God there are straw houses. Oh yeah, you think everything is okay but there is the façade of drugs, the mind-numbing Netflix channel, and dozens and dozens of diversions causing divisions. We have fragile homes that look like fortresses, we have expensive cars and boats that act like our chariots, but the insurance coverage, the retirement plans, the cardboard systems of alarms and home security, are just a few of the thousands of substitutes for 8:28.

When you walk through the door of Romans 8:28, there is true freedom. There is stability and depth. Even though the enemy huffs and puffs and blows all kinds of tragedy and turmoil towards you, your house will not fall. It's not divided. When people really live by 8:28 you can go from the measles to the mortuary, from chicken pox to that cold slab, or from childhood to glory, being and experiencing real, true freedom from the pains of this world. If you cling to 8:28, if you make it your address, if you make it God's promise to you – and it is – then you will live in God's security and it doesn't matter who or what comes

103

knocking at your door. You are at your strongest at 8:28. You desperately need to understand about this promise. It's so good, we need to read it again:

> *And we know that for those who love God all things work together for good, for those who are called according to his purpose.*   *-Romans 8:28*

Three Questions of the Promise:

- Promise is made to whom?
  - Those of Christian Character!

The promise of 8:28 is for the Christ-follower. To Christians. To those justified in Christ. To those who have been impacted by the Resurrection of Christ from the grave. To those who have been adopted or grafted into the Kingdom of God. To those whom God has called. To those sanctified, to those who have bowed their knees to Almighty God in a relationship with Christ... get it? It is not to EVERYBODY!

If you are not a believer, if you have not been called, if you have not turned from your selfish way in repentance to God, then things will not turn out for good. This verse is maybe the most bastardized verse in the Bible. It's been hijacked by nominal believers to soothe their souls from the problems of life. It's become the father of all lies for the person that has ignored and flipped God off for most of their lives. When things go wrong and they start crying and begging for temporary help, some well-meaning friend comes along and says, "It's going to be okay. Don't worry. Things will work out in the end. My pastor says ALL things will work out. God's got this, don't worry, it's okay. God is going to make it all work out for you." And the person takes their shirt sleeve and dries their eyes. They wipe the snot off their nose, and clear their throat, and sit up straight and say, "Yeah, yeah, God's not going to do this to me! He's got me!"

Let me ask you a very serious question, Does He? Does He have you? Does He really have you?

The truth is, as much as this verse gives comfort and strength to me as a Christ-follower, it should terrify those who don't walk with Him. Many have fooled themselves thinking that God does have them, when He doesn't because they haven't repented and bowed down to Him. If you are not a believer, not a Christian, and haven't turned from sin, the very thing that separates you from God, then things are not going to be all right. Things will not turn out for the good — things are going to become catastrophic for you.

My grandmother made breakfast every day for anyone who would come to her house. Every day the meal was complete with eggs, bacon and sausage. She had toast, and every day she had grits. Sometimes salmon patties. And if you were lucky, a few times a year, pig brains to go with your eggs. You are not "country" unless you have eaten pig brains for breakfast. And, and, every day on the table was your choice of toppings for your toast...butter, not spray butter or margarine, real butter. And there was jelly, eight different flavors of jam, and always, always on the table was fig preserves. Oh my goodness, they were good. Usually, she had gone to her brother's house and handpicked those figs because there were some that had already rotted, and she would leave them on the ground. Then she would take the good ones and come home to cook them. They were genuine homemade, and she never ran out. Figs. Please discover the incredible flavor of figs.

In Jeremiah 24, God says to Jeremiah... "Look son, there are two baskets...one with very good figs, and the other with figs so bad that you can't eat them." God said, "Jeremiah, that is the picture of the people of Judah." You see, God allowed Babylon to invade Judah because of the overall unrighteousness of the country. Did you hear me? *Because of the overall, general, far-reaching unrighteous living of the country* As. A. Whole. Are you with me? But Jeremiah, some are like good figs...

> *I'll keep my eye on them so that their lives are good, and I'll bring them back to this land. I'll build them up, not tear them down; I'll plant them, not uproot them.*

"And I'll give them a heart to know me, God. They'll be my people and I'll be their God, for they'll have returned to me with all their hearts.   -Jeremiah 24:6,7

And God continues and says, "But Jeremiah, the bad figs…" It's bad:

I'll make them something that the whole world will look on as disgusting— repugnant outcasts, their names used as curse words wherever in the world I drive them. And I'll make sure they die like flies….   -Jeremiah 24:9

I like the simple comparative analogy of figs… it hits home for me. Here's the deal about 8:28 living… it hits home: character counts, and the only character that counts with God is Christ-like character. 8:28 is the promise of all promises! It's stupendous! It's wonderful… oh my goodness… my life, your life, our life is filled with difficult times and to have this promise tattooed on our hearts: all things work together for good, for everybody, for everything! No, for those in Christ.

- Promise covers what?
    o All Things!

The 8:28 promise covers all things, good and bad. It's comprehensive! All things will work out, will work for, and work in, you – for good. All things. Things that you understand are bad, and things you can't figure out that invade your life. Things that are fair and things that are unfair. Sometimes like stinks and you just can't figure it out... those things. Sometimes it seems that we go through periods where we don't get it and things happen... those things. Sometimes things happen and we don't accomplish much... those things. Sometimes life seems pointless. I mean just last week things were going great, you had a grip, you had understanding, you had your arms wrapped around things, but they slipped and now, what is going on in the world with the things that are happening... those things. We are confused about things and unable to pray... those things. All things, each and every tragedy.

Joseph, the dude with the coat of colors his dad had made for him to show him how much he loved him, was on his way now. It made his brothers mad, they became jealous, they sold him into slavery. So sad, Joseph had so much promise. He was going to become somebody! He had things to do. He worked his way up to the top servant of a guy named Potiphar, who was high up himself in the chain of command under Pharaoh of Egypt. He was on his way now! Yet when Pharaoh's wife made a play for Joseph, he rejected her in favor of living right for God. She cried rape. Joseph was sent to prison. Two of Pharaoh's servants were sent to jail and were in the same cell as Joseph. They had dreams and well, what do you know, Joseph interprets dreams, a gift he had from God. He foretold the future, told Pharaoh's winetaster to get him out of there… whoa, Joseph is on his way… no, the winetaster forgot about Joseph and it was another two whole years. Then Pharaoh had a dream, the winetaster remembered Joseph and now, now, Joseph is on his way. The story is my absolute favorite Old Testament story. Joseph rescues the day, rescues Egypt, rescues the whole starving world, and rescues and restores his whole family life!

And then, then comes that verse at the end of Genesis, in Genesis 50, that makes your mouth drop open. When you read it, you see God. When you read and understand it, you know that God has a plan and God has worked His plan and God is a God of redemption, of salvation. God is on the rescue for you. If you are a believer, then realize through your sweating, your pain and hurt… all things work together for good. You see, Joseph's dad, Jacob, died. It was after the rescue, but Joseph's brothers believed now that their dad was dead, Joseph was faking and now he will really get them. It's the bad rap we put on God sometimes. Here is 8:28 in the Old Testament:

> But Joseph said to them, "Do not fear, for am I in the place of God? As for you, you meant evil against me, but God meant it for good….   -Genesis 50:19

8:28. Evil is meant against you, people forsake you, friends turn on you, relationships go bad, life breaks our hearts, but God is in the heart-healing business. For those who are called, who are *called*… how do you know if you are called? How do you know? What is the sign? You know you are called when you turn to Him. *All things* include your wins and your losses.

- Promise outcome?
  - Good!

> *You don't get wormy apples off a healthy tree, nor good apples off a diseased tree. The health of the apple tells the health of the tree. You must begin with your own life-giving lives. It's who you are, not what you say and do, that counts. Your true being brims over into true words and deeds.*　　　　　　-Luke 6:43-45

There is a conquest envisioned here and it's one of goodness. A lot of us mistake 8:28 for some personal feelings of good. Yes, it is a promise made to us by God for good. But not for some cheap, expendable, brief, temporary, fleeting or momentary jollies. Don't confuse the world's good with God's good. It's not a *feel* good, it's not a *best for me* good.

110

The good that God is talking about in 8:28 is the good where He is going to bring you all the way home. He is going to bring you through doubtful, difficult times. The good God talks about is that *forever* good of being with Him forever. God does have a plan for your life — to rescue you and to bring your life to full glory for Him.

I love the old story of a wealthy man who had only one son, who he loved dearly. The wealthy man was interested in collecting expensive and rare pieces of art. He taught his son to love art as well, and together they began to collect some of the most exquisite pieces of art in the world.

A war broke out and the son was called away to fight. After a few months, the father received word that his son was missing in action and not long after he was notified that his son had been killed. The father's heart was shattered. He had accumulated all of these treasures, but none of them could compare to his only son.

One day, a knock came on the father's door. As he opened the door, he saw a soldier in full uniform. The soldier said, "Sir, I was a good friend of your son. I want you to know that he died trying to save the lives of other people. I am not an artist, but I painted a picture of your son just before he died, and I wanted to give it to you." The father was overjoyed. He had seen better, more quality work, but none of that mattered because this was a portrait of his son.

The father took the painting and put it over the mantle in his home, in the midst of millions of dollars-worth of art.

In time, the old man died. Invitations were sent to come to an auction of the old man's art collection. Many came from around the world to bid on these rare items. As the auction opened the auctioneer started off with the painting of the old man's son. Many of the famous art collectors shouted, "That isn't worth anything. It's the worst painting I've ever seen. We came to see 'real' art. Let's get to the good stuff."

The auctioneer stated that the stipulation of the father's will was that the painting of the son was to be sold first. They started the bidding at $100, but no bids. Then $50, but no bids. Finally, the bidding went to $10 and one of the old man's servants, in the back, said, "I'll give $10 for the painting."

Suddenly, the auctioneer lowered his gavel and shouted, "This auction is officially over!" Cries came back from the crowd, "What do you mean this auction is over?" The auctioneer then informed them that, according to the will of the Father, *"WHOEVER GETS THE SON, GETS IT ALL!"*

- I came to Him a sinner, but He made me a saint
- I came to Him a pauper, but He made me a prince

- I came to Him a child of the devil, but He made me a child of God
- I came to Him in a famine, but He gave me a feast
- I came to Him with grief, but He filled me with glory
- I came to Him in humiliation, but He threw me a celebration
- I came to Him a beggar, but He made me a believer
- I came to Him a victim, but He made me a Victor
- I came to Him fallen, but I left Him fixed
- I came to Him corrupted, but He made me converted
- I came to Him with Him nothing, but He gave me everything
- I came to Him on my way to Hell, but He put me on the road to Heaven
- I came to Him broken, but He healed me
- I came to Him with bad news, and He gave me good news
- I came to Him caving into to this world, but He lifted me out of the pit
- I came to Him doubting, but He gave me hope…hope in Christ

He did it for me, and He will do it for you, if you will come to His fortress, come to His promise, come to His covenant, come to His home...

I've wandered far away from God
Now, I'm coming home
The paths of sin too long I've trod
Lord, I'm coming home.
Coming home, coming home
Never more to roam
Open wide thine arms of love,
Lord, I'm coming home.

Chapter Nine

This is the coolest series I have ever done in going on 29 years as a pastor and preacher. It is a blast! The greatest chapter in the Bible and, last chapter, the greatest verse in the greatest chapter — perhaps the greatest verse of the Bible. And now… the follow up. Listen and read intently, because this world is in major trouble, you are in this world, and you and I walk through these troubling times. What is the answer?

One of the greatest weaknesses in the modern-day American church is that almost no one believes God invests His power in the Bible. If we did, then we couldn't stay out of it! It seems like everyone in the contemporary church is looking for power in a program, in a methodology, in a technique, in anything and everything but that in which God has placed it — His Holy Word. The Word of God alone has the power to change lives for eternity.

In the Old Testament book of Jeremiah there is a tiny little illustration that is tucked away tightly and often missed in our Bible reading and study. I have preached on it several times in the past seven years. It's one of those stories that's not remarkable, just plain, but carries a wallop to our thick skulls. It's one of those Bible truths that it is easy to miss if you are not paying attention.　.

Here it is: God tells Jeremiah to go to the community of the Rechabites, a little group of people on the outskirts of town. Just some country folk. And God says, "Jeremiah, I want you to go to the local church there, the temple, reserve a room and invite the Rechabites, and serve them some wine." All right! A wine tasting! Jeremiah bee-bops on down the short little drive to where the Rechabites lived. They gather… Jeremiah has wine on the table, in gallon jugs! And it's good wine too! Don't think that God's man, receiving orders from God, is going to stop at K-mart and get some MD 20/20, or Boone's Farm, or some Night Train. No, he's getting the good stuff! He puts it on the table, pours it, and says, "Forever to thee!" And the Rechabites just sat there… they were Clemson fans. Listen, you know I'm a Gamecock!

The patriarch speaks up: "We don't drink wine…never have…never will." You see, our grandfather told his children years ago, "Don't ever drink wine. Don't build a house, and don't plant a garden." What does that mean? It means you are a camper! Anyone like camping? Good for you. I'm a hotel guy. I like those sorry continental breakfasts that we seem to fall for as an added bonus every time we check in to a hotel.

For years and years, the Rechabites were obedient to their grandfather and lived a simple life just like he had outlined. Recently, though, they found themselves in the path of Nebuchadnezzar's army and had to move to the outskirts of Jerusalem. No big deal, they love to camp, and they could move in the middle of the night if need be because they were never too drunk to drive.

At this point – it looks immediate in Scripture – as Jeremiah still has his glass in the air and the Rechabites are looking at him like he's lost his mind, God speaks to Jeremiah and says, "Jeremiah! The Rechabites grandfather told them not to drink and they have obeyed totally, completely, and joyfully. No one has been disobedient to that old man! They haven't had a single drop! They have honored their ancestor! There was a game plan. They listened to the plan, and they carried out the plan."

You can read the heartbreak in the words God speaks to Jeremiah about the Rechabites. God set Jeremiah up! Go and throw a little wine party. Their response: We don't drink wine because we honor our grandfather. And God says,

> *But look at you! I have gone to a lot of trouble to get your attention, and you've ignored me. I sent prophet after prophet to you, all of them my servants, to tell you from early morning to late at night to change your life, make a clean break with your evil past and do what is right, to not take up with every Tom, Dick, and Harry of a god that comes down the pike, but settle down and be faithful in this country I gave your ancestors. And what do I get from you? Deaf ears.*
> *-Jeremiah 35:14-16 MSG*

What is going on in the world today? Deaf ears. God has spoken, continuing to withhold His Holy wrath, extending His mercy, yet we won't relent our constant complaining and coveting.

The Rechabites had a plan. There was a chain of command from the top down. No wine, no city living, and no vineyards or gardens. Believe me, I'm not here to preach to you no drinking, quit living in the city, take up camping, and shop for your vegetables at the grocery store. I have something more pressing than that! What Paul says is way more important than that. And in Romans 8:29-30 there are power-packed statements and truths by the Apostle Paul. Let's look at them… let's dip back into last week a little with some 8:28 then go forward:

> *And we know that for those who love God all things work together for good, for those who are called according to his purpose. For those whom he foreknew he also predestined to be conformed to the image of his Son, in order that he might be the firstborn among many brothers. And those whom he predestined he also called, and those whom he called he also justified, and those whom he justified he also glorified.*
> *-Romans 8:28-30*

It's known as the *Golden Chain of Salvation* by scholars. There is a chain of events, a sequence of moves, of commands from God. And here's the deal and how it all relates to the Rechabites: the Golden Chain leads somewhere. There is an iron chain that keeps you and me in bondage to sin, but God has intervened and given us His golden chain of His command to takes us to an ultimate place.

In 8:28 Paul is giving the pre-message to the ultimate message. The ultimate message is that God has a home for us! Forget about the decorations for a moment and realize what God wants us to know. That is: we will be with Him. And our function, our life, will be to glorify Him!

8:28 living is that everything that happens to the believer, no matter how life-shattering you think it is, no matter how absent you feel God is in the situation, and no matter the effects upon your life, will turn out for your good, my good, our good. 8:28 is to 8:29-30 that no matter what happens, God's contract with us through His Son is valid and always will be. Nothing can interrupt it! And let me just give you a peek at what's next:

> *What then shall we say to these things? If*
> *God is for us, who can be against us?*
> *-Romans 8:31*

But here is the key: What is *good*? What does Paul mean? It doesn't mean you are going to get your feelings hurt and then get a new Chevy. It doesn't mean that you will go through bad times from age 20-50 and then get an early retirement, a boat, and the Publisher's Clearing House $5,000-a-week for life. The good that God is talking about is our someday, our eternity, our time after this life. And I don't know if you have checked the calendar lately, but your time is running out. My time is running out! The good Paul is talking about here is that glorification. It's that mansion that Jesus talks about in John 14. Paul is assuring us of the plan.

What is the plan? This passage of Scripture here in verses 29 & 30 is known as the *Golden Chain of Salvation*.

The Golden Chain

- God knows

Nike had commercial success thirty years ago with the slogan, "Bo knows." Bo was Bo Jackson, the Heisman-winning running back at Auburn. He went on to play for the Los Angeles Raiders and was arguably the best back ever, in my opinion. The only reason others wouldn't say it is because he only played three years due to a hip injury. "Bo knows" was a brilliant ad campaign because Bo also played Major League Baseball. Very few have ever played two professional sports. I mean, you can probably count them on one hand. Nike was elevating Bo to this superstar status because of his diversity and capability in two sports. It was like he was a god in sports. He could do two things in professional sports. No, God knows more than Bo. We try to be cool and talk about God in trendy ways, but folks, God knows everything!

Understand the depth of this next statement: There are no rogue molecules in the universe! There is not one single molecule... and you know what a molecule is don't you? It's a group of atoms bonded together, representing the smallest fundamental unit of a chemical compound. And there is not one... not a single one… that is running around and not counted by God. God knows all. If that is not true, then everything we believe about the power of God and His Word is not the truth. All of your faith is based on God knowing everything about you and me. He knows we are sinners, yet He chooses to rescue us despite that ugliness.

> *For you formed my inward parts; you knitted me together in my mother's womb. I praise you, for I am fearfully and wonderfully made.* -Psalm 139:13,14

- ■ God Chooses

This is where some want to get off the train. What do you mean God chooses? Here's where I call a quick timeout. Timeout. When someone says, "I don't believe God chooses, but we get to choose." *If* God doesn't get to choose what He wants, then how in the world is He God? He chose Abraham, and remember, Abraham wasn't one of the chosen Israelites (the family of God), no, Abraham was a scoundrel and reprobate, just like you and me. The Bible says, "Jacob I have loved, Esau, have I hated." There is a choosing in that.

- ■ God Calls

There is this effectual calling of God. Many, many hear the sermons, the evangelistic cries of the preachers and teachers, still they put off that turn from their own ways to God's way. But there is this inner call that can't be denied. I can't explain it. For some it's quick, for others they struggle to come to God – but they do come to Him.

It's so difficult to hear the call these days because the enemy works overtime to occupy our time. Before you know it you are age thirty, you are fifty, or you are seventy, and the saddest words I've ever heard are those words: "I've made it this far like I am so I'll just go the rest of the way and hope it works out." It won't. Is God calling you? Answer Him!

- God Makes it Right

The giant theological word is Justify. It means God makes the relationship right with Him. What is a Christian? It is someone who has heard a call and responded to that call. They respond to the call of repentance – of turning from your sin and turning to God.

Don't be fooled today in this world of American Christianity! It's not about the latest cool dude finding the latest, coolest thing to do on Sunday mornings to entertain us. God makes it right between He and I because of the Cross where Jesus died. Do you think about this: do you think the God of this universe is going to orchestrate the greatest miracle ever, the biggest rescue mission ever, the one that He says, He *says*, can't fail.

"Yeah," God says over and over, "I'm putting my reputation on the line...." Do you think He is going to leave it to you and me to choose Him? God makes *what* right? He declares that we are one in relationship with Him. The term Justification means a legal contract.

- God Glorifies

Everything is about the glorification of Him. In other words it's about worshiping Him, thanking Him, acknowledging Him, praying to Him, thinking about Him. If He does it then what in the world is the problem? Can't you see it? We are a resistant bunch. We are hardheaded.

As God calls you today to the Cross of Jesus Christ... what is He getting from you? Deaf ears? Can't we even pray for a little? Can't we even serve a little? Can't we even invite a few? Can't we even care a little about our neighbor? Can't we even give a little? Can't we even come to church? Can't we even participate? Even pagans like the Rechabites can do the right thing, but folks in modern day America whose grandparents were believers are just leaning on that as if it's going to get them in good with God. The good I'm talking about is that eternal home.

Here's the problem today: look at it... if you are not in Christ, there is not a golden chain in your life, but it's a chain, nonetheless. It's one that has you shackled to sin, and you do everything sin tells you to do while smiling and speaking out of the side of your mouth.

Get loose today from the fetters and manacles of sin by turning to God in a relationship with His Son, Jesus Christ.

Chapter Ten

Why did Jesus die? I guess if you are somewhat astute you can say that the Romans killed Him, or that Pilate washed his hands of it, but really that's what sealed His fate. Maybe you could say the Pharisees got to Him, or it's because of the blundering antics of the disciples. Or... or you could say, somewhat smugly, there is no justice in the world. And yes, I will say that sometimes when I am mad at the government or at a politician. But to say there is no justice in the whole world, is to doubt God and His sovereignty and His rule over everything.

Why did Jesus die?

Because He deserved to.

That's a difficult answer for those thinking in squeaky clean religious, lovey-dovey, terms. For the wages of sin, the Bible says, is death. But wait – Jesus never sinned! Yes, but the Bible says our sins were reckoned to His account. He took on our sin on the Cross. Luther said, *"He was the greatest sinner the world has ever seen."* Yeah, that's right. The Gospel of Jesus Christ. While so many are demanding and searching for the next thing that is going to make them feel more religious, the greatest movement the world has ever seen is a man dying on a tree, taking the place where *we* should hang and bleed out. He did it for you and me.

Think about it soberly right now. Just a moment, before we work our way through the best chapter in the Bible. Just before we go through the motions of taking the cup and the bread remembering. Take just another moment. He died for us… yes, He died for us.

> *What then shall we say to these things? If God is for us, who can be against us? He who did not spare his own Son but gave him up for us all, how will he not also with him graciously give us all things?*
> *-Romans 8:31-32*

Well, if you've never heard it, then it sounds like a great Tweet… *if God is for us, then who can be against us!?* Christians have thrown it out there so much that it is sort of like a catch phrase or our own little cheerleading chant that we say right before battle in life. *"If God is for us, then who can be against us!?"* And that might not be a bad thing. Someone tells you that they just lost in life... they lost their job, they lost a friend, or they lost their way, and you say, "Oh! I understand, but *if God is for us, then who can be against us!"* The world is on the brink of disaster, there is rioting in the streets, chaos in the courthouse, and anarchy on the horizon... you and I need it like we've never needed it before: *If God is for us, then who can be against us!* But don't say it meaninglessly... I believe it was said with passion and force. I believe it was said with meaning and application: If God is for us, then who in the whole world can be against us? It's ludicrous.

But you know what I am going to tell you don't you? Yeah, it's more than that. It's a whole lot deeper than meets the eye. Let me ask something of you: Go deep with God, when you do, He will take you further than you ever thought. Will you? Verse 31 starts the summary phase of this chapter. Paul asks, "What then shall we say to these things?" What things?

The things of verse 1. Also, the things when Paul talks about verse 5... and the things in verse 26 and how the Holy Spirit intercedes for us. And when all things work together for good for those who love God and are called according to His purpose. Those things.

And then Paul answers with asking for not a what, but a who. Look at it again:

If God is for us, who can be against us?

It's an assurance, a promise in the Bible – which the Bible is full of. It's God's guarantee that no one or nothing is as great as our God. I like what the Psalter says in Psalm 106 as he starts out:

> Praise the Lord! Oh give thanks to the Lord, for he is good, for his steadfast love endures forever! Who can utter the mighty deeds of the Lord, or declare all his praise?   -Psalm 106:1-2

Can you name the things God has done just in the last twenty four hours? Just in the last hour? Just in the last five minutes? No one can. If He is on our side, who in the world can confront us? Who can snatch us? Who can destroy us? Who can wipe us out? Who can stand against our God? No one and nothing. You see it's a great cheerleading verse… I love it… I love to say it! If God is for us, then what powerless, impotent, poser and fake so-called god can be against me? None. So, let's look at three things that stand out about these two verses.

- The Father <u>Gave</u> His Love

How is God for us? He loves us, and He didn't hold back anything. I don't have any religious stuff or positive sayings to share with you. However, I think that you and I desperately need to know that Jesus loves us. Jesus loves me. Jesus loves you. Wasn't it that great theologian asked to summarize the Gospel in one sentence… *Jesus loves me this I know, for the Bible tells me so.* Here are two simple things we need to be reminded of:

1. God loves you
2. God is stronger than your enemy

Emperor Maximilian loved *"If God is for us, then who can be against us"* so much that he had it stenciled over his dining room table where he could see it every time he ate. Well… Christians… there are a lot of folks these days who think they have arrived, and are bold enough to stand up to God. It's been happening for years and yet the movements, governments, spirits of the darkness, principalities that you can't see with the naked eye, and enemies in the darkness that are against you, cannot stand up to our God. If He didn't allow it, they would not stand for a second in His presence. So, the enemy attacks you and me. It's not enough for the enemy to see you fall down a few times. He wants to wipe you out. In Job, we find out that Satan walks to and fro, looking not to maim but to destroy. What's against you today?

- COVID-19 is against you
- Communism is against you
- Socialism is against you
- Abortion is against you
- Racism is against you
- Disease & Sickness are against you
- Cancer is against you
- Heart disease is against you
- Aging is against you
- Banks or attorneys may be against you
- Someone today is against you
- Somebody today is against you
- The Enemy is against you

But here's the beautiful deal: God loves you! He is for you! God is stronger than your enemies. And if God is for you, if you are on His side, if you have bowed down to Him as King and Lord in your life, if you serve Him, if you love Him, if you have humbled yourself to Him in a life of service, if you have committed your life to honoring Him and giving to His cause and for His love... and someone comes against you???!!! God help 'em. Oh, God, have mercy on their soul.

- The Father Gave Up His Son

Are you a giver? The famous preacher Charles Spurgeon and his wife would sell, but refused to give away, the eggs their chickens laid. Even close relatives were told, "You may have them if you pay for them." As a result, some people labeled the Spurgeons greedy and grasping. They accepted the criticisms without defending themselves, and only after Mrs. Spurgeon died was the full story revealed. All the profits from the sale of the eggs went to support two elderly widows. Because the Spurgeons were unwilling to let their left hand know what the right hand was doing (Matthew 6:3), they endured the attacks in silence.

Love has been hijacked. We believe love is something we do on the outside for everyone to see, or, we believe love is this feeling that has to come down from way deep inside, and that if you don't accept everything and tolerate everyone's personal feelings then you don't have love… real love. Love is not a word I throw around anymore. Do you really want to know what love is? The Bible repeatedly says that you and I choose our selfish desires over God and His way. Zillions of times a day, we essentially flip God off and say, "bye-bye" to Him. Yet He still, for His reasons – for Him – still loves us and calls us because He foreknew us, and He predestined us. He justifies us and He glorifies us, all because of this verse in verse 32:

*He who did not spare his own Son
but gave him up for us all....   -8:32*

Jesus was praying in the Garden right before He was arrested, tried, and condemned to death, "Father, can we do it another way?" There is no voice from God in Gethsemane. There is no reassurance, nothing floated down from heaven and said, "Stay the course! You can do it! If I'm for you, then who can kill you!" There is no "I love you. I've always loved you!" What does this loving Father do? He hands Him over. He loves His creation so much, He loves you and me so much, that He didn't even spare His Son.

And He was escorted out of Gethsemane on to Calvary, and He walked by faith knowing that what the Father said, He trusted and obeyed. The Son took all of your sin and mine upon Himself and as He moaned and cried, the Father turned His back on the Son. The Father hid His face because He can't look upon sin. The earth got dark in the middle of the afternoon, perhaps because all of creation couldn't look upon the Son with all the sin caked upon Him.

Jesus begins reciting Psalm 22, "My God, My God, why have you forsaken Me?" Not because it's the only one He knew or thought of at the moment, but because the Father had the plan in place from the beginning. You would expect that maybe the Father would give the priestly prayer found in Numbers 6, "The Lord bless you and keep you, the Lord make His face shine upon you...." But no, it was a curse because of sin, "The Lord curse you and be angry with you and hide His face from you and refuse to smile upon you, and give you hell."

The Father gave up the Son, He handed Him over. Jesus was crucified because He deserved to be... because of your sin and mine heaved upon Him. Folks, that is love.

- ## The Father Graciously Gives Us All Things

He who did not spare his own Son but gave him up for us all, how will he not also with him graciously give us all things? -Romans 8:32

Think about it for a moment. The great God that gave up His Son — the Son who lived blameless, but took the blame to the point of death, to death on a Cross, and then rose again. The penalty was paid, the plan executed to perfection, to the letter, to exactly how He wanted it done! Don't you think, then, that He will apply the sacrifice with perfection? It's logical! Don't you think that the Almighty, the Sovereign, who put in every jot and tittle and knows the very hairs on your head — don't you think that He is going to call, and that if He calls, don't you think that He will justify? And if He justifies, won't He glorify... glorify all things? What things?

No, not some new jewelry or clothes or even the grand prize of a new car. No. He's talking about this future life, life that goes on forever beyond what these eyes can see today. You see, as much as you hate COVID-19, and everything that goes along with it, it either causes us to see God more or it causes you to distance yourself from Him more. You will either contemplate eternal things or go after temporal things. You will either draw closer to Him, or you will fall further and further away.

Quit crying and complaining and groaning about this world and how you don't have anything, or how nobody loves you, or it's a bad day, or a bad week, or a bad life. For he who has ears to hear, let them hear, "If God is for us, who can be against us?"

Chapter Eleven

Paul has made these statements:

- You are NOT condemned
- You are FREE in Christ Jesus
- FAITH is the only way to please God
- If the Spirit of God DWELLS in you, you have LIFE
- And, you have been ADOPTED by God
- If you Spirit of God lives in you, then you are a CHILD of God
- Suffering now does not compare with GIORY that is coming
- HOPE in Christ is a guarantee, not a wish
- The Spirit HELPS us when we are weak

- The Spirit PRAYS for us
- ALL things work together for GOOD, to those who love God and are called according to His purpose
- God RESCUES us...He foreknew, He predestined, He called, He justified, and He Glorified

And so now, we move into what I call the landing pattern of Romans 8. It's the 747 of chapters in the Bible. It's the Spruce Goose! The H-4 Hercules of chapters. And Paul is landing this vehicle. And, as he is finishing these holy words of truth to be applied to our lives by the Holy Spirit, he asks a series of unanswerable questions. Yes, you can answer the questions, but your answers, my answers, or any scholar's answers don't add up to much worth talking about. Our vocabulary or our grasp of God can't adequately answer these remarkable questions. Paul, himself, can't answer the questions.

Write this down: Don't water God down. The Hebrew people thousands of years ago wouldn't even pronounce His name because He was so holy. When Moses encountered God at Sinai, God told him to take off his sandals... it's a holy place and a holy moment. When Isaiah had that vision and was teleported to the throne room of God, he said, "I'm a man with unclean lips!" He couldn't watch. When John was transported to the throne room in the Revelation, he says seeing HIM was like standing next to the sun. He couldn't take it. Then, he says, he fell down and played dead. And don't forget that the third commandment deals with our approach to even how we say His name with reverence!

I want to talk about the holiness of God today because it's what is happening in Romans 8, and so it's the burden of my heart. In this casual and flippant and rebellious society we have taken on a wrong posture with our approach to King Jesus. I don't know what did it — the Azuza Street revivals in California a hundred years ago? The Jesus–hippie movement in the 1960's? The emerging church movement? The mega-church movement? I don't know, but I do know the biggest misconception, or maybe the most dangerous false teaching in the church these days, is that Jesus is your pal, your buddy. Oh yes, He is your friend... what a friend we have in Jesus, and God called Abraham friend, but it's the characteristics of a friendship that count. It's the covenant, the promises, the commitment of love — not the wrestling on the floor together, going to the mall, and listening to side two of Led Zeppelin 4 together. One of the biggest fallacies and delusions is that Jesus wants you to join Him every morning with your sandals and Yeti cup and sip coffee with Him on the back porch, contemplating life, coming up with some modern day psychology, and exploring your lack of thrills that should be there to define your life of adventure. Folks, are you serious?

Paul, in getting to the end of the chapter, asks a series of questions. And for us to answer the questions with a simple "no one" or "nothing" without feeling and understanding the depth of these questions is to cheapen the Gospel of Jesus Christ. It demeans, degrades, and devalues God's Holy Word. It denigrates our view of His holiness. In other words, if you can't get this message this morning then, even if you were taken to the throne room of God, He would snuff you out on the spot because of your pride and lack of humility and woe-is-me as you strolled into His presence. In Acts 6, Ananias and Sapphira found out the folly of their little plot to lie to the Holy Spirit... He killed them because of their awful and pathetic approach to the holiness of God.

There's the story of a poor European family who saved for years to buy tickets to sail to America. Once at sea, they carefully rationed the cheese and bread they had brought for the journey. After three days, the boy complained to his father, "I hate cheese sandwiches. If I don't eat anything else before we get to America, I'm going to die." Giving the boy his last nickel, the father told him to go to the ship's galley and buy an ice-cream cone.

When the boy returned a long time later with a wide smile, his worried dad asked, "Where were you?"

"In the galley, eating three ice-cream cones and a steak dinner!"

"All that for a nickel?"

"Oh, no, the food is free," the boy replied. "It comes with the ticket."

God did not spare His Son. He gave Him up sparingly. And if He gave us His Son — the ultimate, the best, the One and only — Paul is saying, "He will give us all these other things! So many are living way beneath the means that God provides. So many of us live way below the blessings of peace and trust in the Lord. Here are the questions in verses 31-35 in the Message translation of the Bible:

- With God on our side like this, how can we lose?
- And who would dare tangle with God by messing with one of God's chosen?
- Who would dare even to point a finger?
- Do you think anyone is able to drive a wedge between us & Christ's love for us?

Does Paul have *anyone* in mind when he says *who*? Perhaps. Maybe enemies of Christ. Maybe the diseases, sicknesses, or trials of life? Maybe ruthless despots and dictators that scream the end of Christianity? Maybe *the* enemy himself, Satan?

Unanswerable questions to an apathetic casual crowd, but when you are passionate about God, and about His plan, and about what is real and what is not, you have to answer with a resounding, "Nobody!" "No one!" and at "No time!" Which brings us to this point: why do you doubt and pout? Why do you moan and complain? Why do you and I live in a bubble of selfishness? Why do we capitulate or surrender when the enemy brushes up against us? I'll tell you why: because you can't say, "No one comes against my God!" I'll tell you why: because you don't realize just how massive our God is. I'll tell you why: because when we hear rumors about UFO's, WWIII, and the Communist Party taking down the crosses of churches in China, the first thing we do is cower and think, "Uh-oh, this is bad, maybe we are done." The reason we fear everyone, but stop short of fearing Jehovah God, is that the first thing that crosses our minds is submission to other gods and the philosophy of this angry society rather than fearing our great Almighty!

These really are unanswerable questions to the faint at heart, but if you really want the answers then hang on! Because Paul doesn't spare us from the truth, and he doesn't mix words. And he doesn't answer them all like a Philadelphia lawyer or a Washington lobbyist or a demonstrator against our government.

Answers to the Unanswerable Questions:

With God on our side like this, how can we lose?

- God didn't & doesn't hesitate to rescue you

You know when you ask someone a question and they hesitate just a slight second, and you wonder if they are telling the truth? You know that moment of awkward silence as they blurt out their so-called truthful answer? You know that scene from Seinfeld when Elaine gets the message about her boyfriend being in an accident and she's at the movies and hesitates to go to the hospital, then stops to get some Jujyfruits? The boyfriend figures it out and they break up. Then there's that scene in Shawshank Redemption that says, "If I am going to move on this there can't be the slightest hesitation." God does not hesitate!

Think about this: you and I are sinners. We are not sinners because we sin, rather we sin because we *ARE* sinners! It's our nature! The entire Gospel is based on the premise that you and I are unable to help ourselves. If you are asked to rescue someone (and it's happened to me) — let's say a family member is in jail, or is caught in a crime, and you are called to bail them out – what do you do? I don't know about you, but let me be the one to tell the truth first. I'm going to hesitate and think about it. I'm going to get a cup of coffee, wake up, talk about it, think about it, weigh the differences if I let the scoundrel stay in the jail cell. So if I am asked to bail out, to save, to rescue an enemy of mine – someone who has turned their back on me, someone who has repeatedly messed me up – don't you think my hesitation, reluctance, and unwillingness is justified? Of course it is. I don't know everything.

Now let me give you the answer to this unanswerable question and this is why it's unanswerable: HE DIDN'T HESITATE! He did not spare His Son, but rather He gave Him up. He knows everything, He knows your sin and mine. Yet He did not spare Him, He did not hesitate, He willingly gave Him up.

God called Abraham to sacrifice his son, Isaac, to the Lord. All the way up the mountain to the site of the altar, you have to think that it is playing in the mind of Abraham: *Is God really speaking to me? Is this real? Can I trust God? What will others think of me?* Surely, the enemy was trying to get Abraham to doubt God. But something miraculous happens, something amazing when it comes to obeying God. Look at it:

> *So Abraham rose early in the morning, saddled his donkey, and took two of his*

young men with him, and his son Isaac. And he cut the wood for the burnt offering and arose and went to the place of which God had told him. On the third day Abraham lifted up his eyes and saw the place from afar.

Did you see? The third day? This scene closely mirrors and prophesies the sacrifice of Jesus on the Cross for our sins. All of it unfolds on the third day. Life is given on the third day. How? Because Abraham didn't hesitate to trust God, and God is the giver of life.

And Abraham took the wood of the burnt offering and laid it on Isaac his son. And he took in his hand the fire and the knife. So they went both of them together. And Isaac said to his father Abraham, "My father!" And he said, "Here I am, my son." He said, "Behold, the fire and the wood, but where is the lamb for a burnt offering?" Abraham said, "God will provide for himself the lamb for a burnt offering, my son."

And the Bible says they went from there together and stopped some ways off, and Abraham piled up the wood and bound his son and put him on the wood.

There is no hesitation whatsoever in this language, in this text.

> *Then Abraham reached out his hand and took the knife to slaughter his son. But the angel of the Lord called to him from heaven and said, "Abraham, Abraham!" And he said, "Here I am." He said, "Do not lay your hand on the boy or do anything to him, for now I know that you fear God, seeing you have not withheld your son, your only son, from me." And Abraham lifted up his eyes and looked, and behold, behind him was a ram, caught in a thicket by his horns. And Abraham went and took the ram and offered it up as a burnt offering instead of his son.*
> *-Genesis 22:3-13*

Why did God bless Abraham? Because He knew He could trust Abraham to obey Him. Can God do the same with you? When you read the Word of God and see where it clearly outlines righteous living, do you hesitate? God doesn't hesitate with His love.

And who would dare tangle with God by messing with one of God's chosen?

- The One who died for me – the One raised for me

Is this really an answer to the question? Yes it is. God tangled with sin and death by giving His Son to die on the Cross, and then He raised Him from the clutches of this world. The only adequate answer to any question you have about God is, *Jesus is the One who died for me*. The reason is because the question is always going to be: Who is going to rescue you? Who is going to come for you? Who is going to go to battle against Satan? Who is going to stand in the gap, be the sacrifice, and be your only true friend. He's the One who died for me and the One who raised me. The grave couldn't hold Him because it had nothing to hold Him on! Look at this same question and answer in the ESV:

> *Who shall <u>bring any charge</u> against God's elect? It is God who justifies.*
> *-Romans 8:33*

"Bring a charge" — it's a legal term. Paul's point is not that the enemy won't file charges and bring up those charges while lying about a bunch of charges against the Son. No. The Accuser, that's Satan, will accuse you and lie about you and remind you of your past sin and try to get you to feel guilty and try to get you to quit and surrender and throw in the towel of life.

You can actually read the passion of Paul in this passage. This is how you know God is speaking to you instead of the enemy: God never accuses. The enemy has one plan, one line — it's the lie and line of accusation. Let him go ahead and accuse, but don't buy it! You have been pardoned, freed, and you are innocent before the Almighty. Paul is alluding to Isaiah 50 here:

> But _the Lord God helps me_; therefore I have not been disgraced; therefore I have set my face like a flint, and I know that I shall not be put to shame. He who vindicates me is near. Who will contend with me? Let us stand up together. Who is my adversary? Let him come near to me. Behold, _the Lord God helps me_; who will declare me guilty?   -Isaiah 50:7-9

When the enemy attacks you I promise you that it will not do any good to say, "Hey, I'm a Baptist or I'm a Methodist." It will not help you to say, "I am a member of this church." I promise you, I promise you it will not gain you any advantage to say, "I was christened, confirmed, went through catechism, and baptized when I was eight." I assure you, I pledge to you, I swear to you that saying, "I've been a member of this church for fifty years" doesn't make the enemy sweat. None of that bothers Satan. Only this: "Jesus died for me and rose again, and He declared me free and I am free!" He hates that answer because there is power in it. There is power in freedom from sin.

Who would dare even to point a finger?

- He is at the right hand of God – He is interceding for us

I know, again, this doesn't sound like a direct answer, but it is. The truth is the enemy is successful at pointing his finger of accusation and guilt at you if you don't pray. He is winning in your life if you have shirked prayer. If you have punted quiet time and kicked away kneeling to God, then you are subject to hating that finger. Satan gives you the finger every day. He points it at you!

The true man or woman of God is heartsick today and greatly disturbed and desperately concerned about the prayerlessness of the local church. If you are not praying, then you cannot win the battle against the enemy. If you are not seeking Him, if you are not submitting to God, if you are not humbling yourself before our Almighty and Sovereign Lord, then the enemy is flipping his crooked finger in your face all day long.

If I could hear Christ praying for me in the next room, I would not fear a million

enemies. Yet distance makes no difference. He is praying for me!
-Robert Murray McCheyne

The truth is that "Thank God" the Holy Spirit intercedes for us. Remember Romans 8:26? The Holy Spirit intercedes. He prays for us! Now we see here that Jesus, the Son, the Resurrected One, who has ascended to the right hand, sitting at the right hand, is interceding for us. He goes to God on your behalf. So, in the long haul and scope of things, you can't be blamed. It's all smoke and mirrors from the enemy. He is bringing up stuff that God doesn't remember, or see any more, about your life. Why? You've been raised to life, to really live, not still laying down in death.

I've got a fourth question, oh, but it's too big to answer quickly. We'll get to it in the next chapter.

Years ago, when I was a little boy, my neighbor down the street had a sister… and he wasn't nice to her at all. He was older, and he was taller, and he was intimidating to her. He knew he couldn't hit her or fight her because he was bigger, and his parents would not allow it. But when she made him mad or got in his way, he would simply point his finger in her face and stare at her. She lost their mind! That little finger in her face and that cold stare of accusation, and she couldn't handle it! She would cry and cry and hide and run to her mom or dad. The power my friend had was in accusing. Even when he wasn't going to do anything and he wouldn't harm her physically, he could affect her emotionally. I often wondered what would have happened if that little girl would have laughed in my friend's face. Just laughed and walked off. He couldn't have handled it.

When you realize that God is always on your side and always has been, when you understand that God laughs in the face of the enemy in his accusations, when you understand that our great God is Sovereign, King, and nothing intimidates Him, then to God, <u>may you</u>:

- Not HESITATE to trust Him
- Realize the Holy Spirit is the HELPER
- Understand that HE sits at the right HAND of God talking about you

Chapter Twelve

Nothing separates us from God!

> *Who shall separate us from the love of Christ? Shall tribulation, or distress, or persecution, or famine, or nakedness, or danger, or sword? As it is written,*
>   *"For your sake we are being killed all the day long; we are regarded as sheep to be slaughtered."*   *-Romans 8:35,36*

Separation. Do you like that word? I don't. It's not a good word. It's the fourth question that the Apostle Paul asks in this summation and synopsis of Romans 8. We said something very important last time: when you come to Christ, you get it all! Romans 8 is describing the package deal.

These days they have all-inclusive package deal vacations. Before you even go, you buy your package. They have different levels. For the economy minded, you get the tickets and an every-other-day pass for the pool and a continental breakfast. For the economy plus, you get a whopping two-inch increase in leg room! For the deluxe, you get every day at the pool, continental breakfast, and one extracurricular activity on the island. For super deluxe, you get everything mentioned beforehand, and dinner with the captain. For diamond platinum... and by this time you are sick of scrolling through and keeping up with the benefits of your package. You get the picture, don't you?

In Romans 8, Paul says you get all of Jesus! You get all of God's best. There are no levels of rescue with God. You are included, you are adopted, you are counted, and you are given the guarantee of hope – the hope in Christ and Christ alone. It's the super-deluxe, gold, diamond, platinum plus package. It's everything and more than you have ever dreamed of or are able to think of.

> Now to him who is able to do far more
> abundantly than all that we ask or
> think, according to the power at work
> within us, to him be glory in the church
> and in Christ Jesus throughout all

generations, forever and ever. Amen.
-Ephesians 3:20,21

And now, not only are we reminded of the all-inclusive trip we are on and are going on – yep, one day, you will get on that train and ride it, and ride it to glory – but we are also reminded and guaranteed that our ticket cannot be cancelled. It's non-refundable. And this point is indispensable to your life. The trip of the Christian life is going to take place regardless of the circumstances and no matter how much the gates of hell want to advance against it.

These questions have been rhetorical. They are unanswerable, intending to advance the guarantee of God's agenda and plan. Yet the Christ-follower can answer them! No one, nothing. Not tribulation, distress, persecution, famine, nakedness, danger, nor the sword. None of these things, nor anything else you want to throw against God, will snatch you out of His hands. So here's the natural question we all think about and ask often: "Does God really love me? Because all these bad things are happening to me." Does God really care because if He did then why am I going through this junk? I swear, if God really loved me then I wouldn't be experiencing these tough things. Why do bad things happen to me? I'm a pretty good person. I haven't killed anyone, raped anyone, or thrown any rocks through glass windows. I haven't stolen any money of any significant amount. So why do I have such a hard time?

At first glance of verse 35, "What shall separate me from the love of God?" you would think I have the wrong message. No, I have the right one. It's just that the deep answer is exactly what you need today. Hold on to those questions until a little later. The fact is, some are very separated from God – they're way off! Some are a little closer. Some are not too far off. Others are just a few feet away, but still need to come to Him. And still others know Him, and are in Him, and He is in you. Look at what it says in Paul's letter to the Ephesians:

> But now in Christ Jesus you who once were far off have been brought near by the blood of Christ.   -Ephesians 2:13

Some of you have been brought near to Christ but for some reason, yesterday, today, maybe tomorrow, you feel like you are ten thousand miles away from Him. And when those doubts start to creep into your trust in Him, because you can't get answers to your questions, they cause your relationship with Him to feel like the Grand Canyon is between you and God. So, how much space is between you and God? Have you slid over only a few inches, or is there enough space between you and God to build an Amazon Fulfillment Center?

For some unknown reason, Paul chooses to mention seven things that get between us and God. Because at this point, you and I are saying, "Wait — I love Jesus, and the Bible tells me He loves me too, but why am I feeling this contradiction of love? I thought, you thought, and the world thinks that if God exists and He is in my life then I must be wealthy, and guarded from sickness of any kind, and smiling all of the time, and joyful and looking forward to my next vacation. It's our default question and dilemma whenever bad things happen to us — <u>we doubt that God is near</u>.

And then to top it all off, whenever we are hurting, dying inside, suffering, and feeling immense pain, we begin to think that God's love toward us has grown cold. He's mad. He's disappointed, and now the time has come for Him to punish me, and so this is what punishment and the wrath of God feels like. That's exactly where our thoughts live. All right. These seven things that can make us feel like we are separated from God:

1. Tribulation – Whoa! Such a big Bible

word! It feels like lightning bolts are coming down out of heaven with fire and brimstone! But it's not. It's a fun Greek word to say, "Thlipsis" and it means pressure, or hemmed in, or restricted, or constricted, or left without options. My son called me last week. A member of an organization he is associated with had committed suicide. Suicide is on the rise during the pandemic. Why? Because folks feel like they are out of options. They feel hemmed in. And when our backs are against the wall we either fight or give up, or we let God fight for us. Interestingly, in this world that seems to have all the answers when it comes to prosperity and politicians, we are left cold and feeling out of options when we are far from God.

2. Distress – Ah... this Greek word isn't as fun. *Stenochoria* means to be limited by narrowness. Okay, now we are sensing the picture that Paul is painting for us. We feel like we are confined, out of options, and the space is narrow. You can't maneuver in narrow spaces. You can't make any turns. You can't get comfortable. Here's what Paul is saying: even when you feel confined and tied up and there is nothing you can do to right it... not even that will cause God to leave you.

3. Persecution – The Greek work is "Diogmos"... it means to be hunted down like an animal. It's what is going on in our world today.

Those who know their Bible should not be surprised at the state of the world as it is.
-Martin Lloyd-Jones

158

It's not enough for haters just to laugh at Christians. It's not enough to tell us that we can't talk about Jesus in the city square or in the marketplace. It's not enough that they have totally redefined our vocabulary. It's not enough that they make laws forbidding anyone to preach or actively crusade in the name of Jesus.

Nero used those first Christians as human torches, set Rome on fire, played his fiddle while it burned, and then blamed the Christians. And now, two thousand years later, the church is being shut down. Whether you believe churches need to shut down for COVID-19's sake or not — and I'm not arguing that, because it depends on the severity of the outbreak — the enemy is using it as a tremendous opportunity to attack the church.

God took the dude in the first century that was hunting down Christians like dogs (Saul who became Paul) and turned him into the biggest crusader for the cause of our Lord, for the Gospel. Even being hunted down like dogs doesn't change God's mind or separate us from Him.

4. Famine – No one here has ever experienced anything like famine. Everybody here has eaten way too many meals. We have seen the scenes on TV of starvation in Africa or India. The truth is churches are at fault for starving believers and Christ-

followers of the Word of God. We are starving for Jesus in America while sitting amongst the greatest givers of spiritual nutrition. Churches and Christians are starving for the true Word of God because we would rather get more numbers and be known as the hip church rather than making disciples. The roosters are coming home to roost. The discipleship–cold contemporary church has no answer for the things going wrong in the world today. Our cool approach to God has no answer for the things going wrong in modern society. Our facetious rendering of worship and fake prayer and pitiful trust and faith in God have no answer for the things going wrong in our lives. We are fat on the things of the world, yet we are starving for what is real. Only a relationship with Christ is real. Everything else will turn you out to a dead-end street and pay off with counterfeit cash.

You and I need to put the Cross before us and the world behind us. With the Cross before us, which demonstrates God's grace and mighty love to those in dire need, it is just natural to expect His supernatural gracious spirit will not be withheld from those who are close, to Him.

5. Nakedness – I'm not surprised that naked is in this category. Go back to the Garden to when Adam and Eve sinned against God. Eve ate some

of the fruit of the forbidden tree and immediately, immediately, in Genesis 3:7…

> …and she also gave some to her husband who was with her, and he ate. Then the eyes of both were opened, and they knew that they were naked. And they sewed fig leaves together and made themselves loincloths. -Genesis 3:6,7

Nakedness in open places is shame. And the first time we learn what naked is, and all about, it is describing separation from God. Now, several thousand years later, the Apostle Paul takes us to that point and says not even nakedness causes God to be far from you!

6. Danger – Danger is danger. Peril is peril.

When you are in Christ, there is no danger of you being separated from Christ. Jesus tells the parable of the seeds and the sower. Some fell on the path, fallow ground, and Jesus says that it is the enemy that comes and steals them away. But understand, the seed hasn't taken root. It's a dangerous thing to play around with God and think that you are in Christ. But when we *are* in Christ… look at the reassuring words from the Lord Himself:

My sheep hear my voice, and I know them, and they follow me. I give them eternal life, and they will never perish, and no one will snatch them out of my hand. My Father, who has given them to me, is greater than all, and no one is able to snatch them out of the Father's hand.
-John 10:27-29

Paul is asking this question that is unanswerable by unbelievers, but by believers it is answered: Who can separate us from the love of the Father? NO ONE! NOTHING! NO TIME! NO WHERE!

7. Sword – It's not a large sword but it's a weapon of war, a shorter sword. It's descriptive of destroying peace. Isn't that the plan of the enemy? No, not even that – not even if you are feeling unsettled and unrestful today – not even that will separate you from God. Look at all seven:

- Tribulation
- Distress
- Persecution
- Famine
- Nakedness
- Danger
- Sword

Okay Pastor, I've got it. You've made the point. Nothing separates us from the love of God. So, why do bad things happen to good people? The people of the Old Testament always struggled and were perplexed trying to figure out the reason for their trials. And, here, it kind of looks like there is this throwaway verse. As much as I want to skip over some things in the Bible because I don't think that they mean that much to me, I always find that it's in those verses that God is speaking the loudest to me. Here's another one in verse 36. We get to this point and Paul throws in there a single verse out of the Psalms. Psalm 44 to be exact. Look at it:

> As it is written, "For your sake we are being killed all the day long; we are regarded as sheep to be slaughtered.
> -Romans 8:36

WHAT IN THE WORLD IS HE TALKING ABOUT? We know that suffering and going through stuff is a natural and expected part of the Christian life. Are you being squeezed into a narrow emotional confinement, stressed out, hungry, feeling vulnerable, looking down the barrel of danger and the sword in this world in 2020… guess what? The God in the mirror of your faith is closer than you think! And the opposite is also true. if you are sailing along in a no pain, much gain, hedonistic lifestyle of pain avoidance and pleasure seeking… then that is when I would be scared to death. If money or riches is your god then, you can bank on it, God is far, far away. If power and sexual prowess are your treasure, then be alarmed and frightened because God is not even close. If you have said no to Him, and He still calls you and pleads with you but you have made up your mind to try and do things yourself, you are in great danger. Not because the enemy is close, but because God is far. God's wrath, many times, is the horrible ramification of your bad decision to go the other way.

As Paul is reminding us who God is and what He has done, he is saying, "Do you feel far away from God because of attacks from others?" Forget that! He is close by you! He is in you! You are in Him! There is nothing man made or demonically orchestrated that separates us from God's great love for us. Go to Him! Cry out to Him for rescue from your difficult times. Let Him melt your heart in order for Him to fashion your heart after God.

Are you a Christ-follower, yet you are hurting and suffering? Then it means you are living because our Savior suffered and died. And for the Christ follower, we too, must suffer in this world, and we are going to leave this old decaying body behind. Suffering is only for a season, and it may be a long season, but He is with you when you turn to Him.

Chapter Thirteen

We have pressing matters with Romans 8:37:

> *No, in all these things we are more than conquerors through him who loved us.*
> *-Romans 8:37*

I suppose that, a while back, I used to like superheroes shows and movies. Batman was every boy's favorite in the 1960's. And I remember distinctly the hype when *Superman: The Movie* came out in 1978. That was a big deal and maybe the start of modern superhero movies. Then it was *Batman* in 1989. I wish I had collected Superman comic books!

Who knew how much they'd be worth? In 2014, a 1938 Superman comic book that sold for 10¢ went for $3.2 million — the highest ever paid for a comic book. I've seen the Spiderman movies, at least two of them, and I've seen an Ironman or two, and I really liked the Black Panther movie. Superheroes are cool. It's fun to watch how they supersede the laws of gravity and the laws of nature.

The word for conqueror here in verse 37 is "hupernikao." Understand that this is not the word for conqueror, it's one word for the compound, "more than conqueror." It's not just winning, it's winning by going away with no one to challenge you. It's winning a football game by a hundred touchdowns. It's scoring five hundred points in a single basketball game. It's playing a major league baseball game and scoring a hundred runs in the first inning… there is no use in playing the other eight innings. Paul says we are not only victors, but way more than that. Now, we can go back to verse 31 and understand it a little more, "If God is for us, who can be against us!" It's uneven. It's not fair for them. And do you remember last chapter? You get all of this! It's yours. Paul says, *"we"* are "more than conquerors." Hold on to that…let's have some fun and talk about superheroes. Let's look at a few, just a few, of some of the most incredible men of the Bible whom God used and displayed His power through and to.

Noah

The world was a corrupt mess. It was chaotic. Read those cryptic verses in Genesis 6 and you see some funky stuff.

> *The Nephilim were on the earth in those days—and also afterward—when the sons of God went to the daughters of humans and had children by them. They were the heroes of old, men of renown.*
> *-Genesis 6:4*

Nephilim were thought of as giants. The only other reference is Numbers 13. Look at that, "heroes of old." Look at the next few verses:

> *The Lord saw that the wickedness of man was great in the earth, and that every intention of the thoughts of his heart was only evil continually. And the Lord regretted that he had made man on the earth, and it grieved him to his heart. So the Lord said, "I will blot out man whom I have created from the face of the land, man and animals and creeping things and birds of the heavens, for I am sorry that I have made them." But*

Noah found favor in the eyes of the Lord.
-Genesis 6:5-8

So, the world had some kind of wicked supermen, or something like it, roaming the earth. The issue is they were evil. It's the same in modern day comic books. It's the same with Ironman, or Superman, or the newest one, Black Panther. Every superhero has a nemesis. That's the premise of every superhero movie. There is always a bad guy.

Noah is God's superhero! Why? God chose him. Folks, that's enough. So many people want to try and figure out God's motives and what God is thinking and why this is happening… God is God! That's why. It's the problem in Christianity today, we've made ourselves the center of the universe and want to use God as our errand boy.

God is going to destroy the world with a flood. Noah is tapped to build a boat. Do you see it? It's this fantastic superhero-looking picture, where God is painting Himself to be the Rescuer! The flood is covering the entire earth. That means that there is no escape. There is nowhere to hide, no safety zones, no food, no medicine, nothing. God and God alone is the rescuer.

Someone calculated it according to the ages given of Noah's sons, Shem, Ham, and Japheth, and said Noah was about five hundred years old when he started building the boat. Folks, this is superhero stuff!

They calculate it took anywhere from fifty-five to seventy-five years to build it. You have to think, it was Noah building it all by himself.

The modern world has a difficult time believing this! God bless the man that has built the exact replica of the Ark in Ohio for a tourist attraction. God is super! He's not superman though. He's not a man. He is super beyond our comprehension, and He is holy. Noah completes the boat, he loads it up with the animals, male and female, loads the supplies and the Bible says God shuts them in there. For forty days it rained and flooded the earth. Noah, he could have been the first superhero.

Daniel

You talk about a superhero... oh my goodness. Stuck to a regimented diet of vegetables and water for ten days, and his appearance of health was noted. He interpreted Nebuchadnezzar's dream. He was promoted up the ladder in a foreign government. He interpreted the vision of Nebuchadnezzar. Then Darius came to the throne and the people worshiped him. But not Daniel! Even though he was high up in government, he still worshiped God and God alone. The senators and other governors wrote a law that for thirty days no one was to worship any god except Darius, and the punishment was to be thrown into the hungry lion's den.

Think about this for a minute. Why just thirty days of worshipping Nebuchadnezzar only? Ever heard of the 21/90 rule? It takes something twenty-one days to become a habit and ninety days for a lifestyle change. Thirty days was probably their introduction for this becoming permanent. Do you think that Satan shows up in a red suit and a pitchfork and jumps on top of a skyscraper and says, "I'm closing down the churches! I'm outlawing prayer! I'm throwing anyone in jail and throwing away the key if they worship God!"?

Nope. I'll tell you how he does it. Ohh… "there is a pandemic," he says to himself. "Okay, while they are caught off guard trying to figure out how to have school, Starbucks, and college football, we will make things a little more aggravating and close the churches. Just for a few weeks, just so everyone will be safe." We buy it, and I'm telling you, the next virus, the next pandemic, they come up with another excuse. Until they eliminate it. I've told you, it's happening in China, and it's happening under our noses even in California. Our government is wanting to eliminate church.

Nothing interrupts Daniel's time with the Lord. Do you have a schedule like that with God? Or, does Facebook take priority over your time with God? Does something that just comes up interrupt your time with God? Will you put off spending time with God in His Word or on your knees because you were invited to go shopping or to the game? Daniel won't, and doesn't.

When Daniel knew that the document had been signed, he went to his house where he had windows in his upper chamber open toward Jerusalem. He got down on his knees three times a day and prayed and gave thanks before his God, as he had done previously. Then these men came by agreement and found Daniel making petition and plea before his God. Then they came near and said before the king, concerning the injunction, "O king! Did you not sign an injunction, that anyone who makes petition to any god or man within thirty days except to you, O king, shall be cast into the den of lions?" The king answered and said, "The thing stands fast, according to the law of the Medes and Persians, which cannot be revoked."

-Daniel 6:10-12

Do you know the rest of the story? They hauled him off, throwing him into the Lion's Den. This isn't Barnum and Bailey's drugged up cats in a cage with someone outside with a gun. No, it's a hole in the ground where they have probably ten or more massive cats, and where they throw them a side of bloody beef every other day, and they all fight to get a bite. Daniel is thrown in, and the door is shut, and everybody clears out, because you don't want to hear the bloodcurdling screams coming from the other side. The next day, they opened the door. Darius called out into the dark, "Daniel, are you okay?" Daniel said, "King Darius, I hope you live forever, this is no big deal. God shut the lion's mouths." He must have been a superhero.

Job

Strange. Why didn't I pick David? Why not Elijah and all the miracles he did? Job? Yes, Job. He was the Bill Gates of his time. He had the status of LeBron. He was as famous as the Beatles. He was superstar status in his own quiet little way. And he lost it all. All of it was taken from him. What makes Job a superhero? His friends traveled a great distance to come sit and cry with him, and then they accused him. His wife told him to curse God and die. There was the burden of mourning the loss of his children, and how was he going to live? How would he eat? Where was he going to live? Yet when the dust cleared, one thing was for certain. He trusted God. You have to be a superhero in faith to trust God when all of your possessions and family that define you are taken away. And after that tough reminder from God, all his possessions were restored, he was richer than before, his trust in God secure and solid as a rock. After it was all over, look at Job's response,

I know that you can do all things....
                                        -Job 42:2

All things work together for good to those who love God and are called…. If God is for us who can be against us? For we are more than conquerors in Christ Jesus. Job – a superhero. Not because he flew through the air, or did these elaborate miracles like Elijah or Elisha, or traveled in time like Philip, or called down all of heaven like Moses, or healed the crippled like Peter and John. No, Job was a hero because he *never* gave up on God. It's those kinds of heroes we need today in this world.

So, this is what Romans 8:37 is all about? Superheroes of the Bible? Sort of. We get it all when we come to Christ. The impossible has happened. In our disobedience and sin, and flipping off God regularly, and being apathetic and forgetful of Him, not thanking Him, not acknowledging Him, not serving Him, not turning to Him, not praying to Him, not seeking Him, not giving, not really living, and thirsting and whoring after more stuff that makes us giggle for a few moments because we have more than our neighbors… because of all that, there is a God who sent His Son to rescue you from your hurts, habits and hang-ups.

And today, it's important to realize the superstar, hero status he is talking about. In Ezekiel 14 it's the same problem then as it is today – they were idol worshipers. We do the same. We worship money, entertainment, sports, hobbies, travel, vacation, health, you name it, we worship it. God had enough of it. He said, 'Ezekiel, tell them that because of their faithlessness, I'm sending judgment on them... sword, famine, wild animals, and pestilence.' And folks, here's where the superheroes come in:

> ...even if these three men, Noah, Daniel, and Job, were in it, they would deliver but their own lives by their righteousness, declares the Lord God.   -Daniel 14:14

> ...even if these three men were in it, as I live, declares the Lord God, they would deliver neither sons nor daughters. They alone would be delivered, but the land would be desolate."   -Verse 16

> ...though these three men were in it, as I live, declares the Lord God, they would deliver neither sons nor daughters, but they alone would be delivered. -Verse 18

> ... even if Noah, Daniel, and Job were in it, as I live, declares the Lord God, they

*would deliver neither son nor daughter.
They would deliver but their own lives by
their righteousness.   -Verse 20*

Why is Romans 8:37 about superheroes and more than conquerors and super-victors? Because of Jesus.

*No, in all these things we are more than
conquerors through him who loved us.*
                                        -Romans 8:37

Noah, Daniel, and Job were great, righteous-living dudes, but they can't save you. Elisha, Elijah, and David were incredible men, but they didn't die for you. Abraham, Isaac, and Jacob were the fathers of the nation that were the forerunners of the church, but they can't rescue you. Peter, James, and John; Samson, Deborah, and Ruth; Esther, Phoebe, and Rahab — they saved people! They rescued God's people at that time. It was their job! But they can't save you or me or anyone else from eternal damnation.

If there is one thing this world needs today — it needs to be saved, to be rescued. The church today may be down, and the referee has started counting. The statistics say we close thirty churches a week, maybe more now that COVID is here. Christians are being persecuted and killed now more than any time in history. They are burning Bibles — not seventy-five years ago in Nazi Germany, not in the streets of Iran, not in North Korea – on the very streets of America, as we sit by and watch. The enemy keeps predicting the demise of the Church and they keep crucifying our Lord over and over. AND the blood is still good for today, and the blood still forgives those who are the meanest and most despicable.

And for those of you, of us, who have been called of Christ, justified, and glorified, the Bible says we are more than conquerors, more than just ordinary heroes. We are more than the likes of Superman, and Spiderman, and Ironman, who rescue someone from getting hurt or dying. We, who belong to Christ – because He is the hero of heroes, because He is the King of Kings, because He is the Lord of Lords – we are in Him, Paul says, and we are more than conquerors. Winning is everything for the Christian. The only thing.

Chapter Fourteen

We introduced it with verses 35 and 36: separation. And in many cases, it is not good. Social scientists, especially child psychologists, often talk about separation anxiety. It's a normal stage of development for infants and toddlers. It's the distress of separation felt by a child when they are apart from their parents. Most children grow out of it. But if not, they say, it becomes separation anxiety disorder. They say it complicates things. It becomes panic in older children and teenagers. Then it can turn into a phobia or an obsessive-compulsive disorder.

Romans 8 has been a fantastic study for us. We have been exposed to the deep things of God. In 14 chapters we have learned some fantastic things. We began in verse one and found out that there is no condemnation for those who are in Christ Jesus. Today, as we close the series and look at the last two verses, we see that there is no separation. From no condemnation to no separation. Praise God.

Pastor, why is this important? Because the thoughts that go through our minds daily are those of:

1. "Am I really rescued?"
2. "Does God remember my sins?"
3. "Is God still going to punish me?"
4. "Because I was bad, God is getting even."
5. "I hope I'm going to heaven."
6. "I feel God is far, far away from me."
7. "I'm not good enough to be a Christian."

This is what I call it:

Spiritual Obtuse Separation Anxiety Disorder

SO SAD.

You see, those questions and comments, plus a billion more, are wrapped around these two points Paul makes. It's sad, so sad to let yourself think you are separated even for one second from God. There is no condemnation and there is no separation. Now, we *should* be condemned because we are rebels against

God in our sin. We *should* have to pay the price for our own sins. We *should* be separated miles and miles and light-years and light-years from the holiness of God. But *because of Jesus* we can draw near to God. Very near. Because of God's mercy we can get close up. Right beside. And the Scriptures even say we are "In Him." You can't get any closer than that.

Let's look at separation today and the fact that we can't be separated from God when we are in Christ. Because it's sad, *SO SAD,* that we let ourselves be fooled into living somewhere in the middle where it never gets comfortable. We can't be separated from God. Do you get that? We can't. We may act like it, but we can't, because this passage of Scripture and the closing thought of Romans 8, the greatest chapter in the Bible is one of assurance! And with all the goings-on in this wild and crazy world today, you don't need money, a gun, a wall, or a slick, lying politician. What you and I need now, at this stage of our lives and in our relationship with Jesus, is an assurance. And this is it:

> *For I am sure* *that neither death nor life, nor angels nor rulers, nor things present nor things to come, nor powers, nor height nor depth, nor anything else in all creation, will be able to separate us from the love of God in Christ Jesus our Lord.*
> *-Romans 8:38-39*

There is a spiritual nature to the list. Paul doesn't say that your drinking buddies can't separate you from God. Paul doesn't say your bad habits keep you from God. Paul doesn't say your job, your vacations, your spending habits, your car, your Internet time, your time spent playing video games. Paul doesn't mess with the stuff that we think of normally. He says *death* and *life*, *angels* and *rulers*. Rulers would be that word for the spiritual realm. Look at the word, "powers." It also has a mysterious spirit world connotation. Paul is living in the first century A.D. The times were changing. People were moving on from Greek mythology and the Roman gods like Zeus and Apollo. The world was embracing Eastern religions and astrology. We do the same today. Paul is literally going into and out of this world to tell us that the love of Christ is more powerful than *anything* you can think of, name, or imagine.

Now, let me jar your memory. Paul listed seven things that can't separate us from God. Remember? Tribulation, distress, persecution, famine, nakedness, danger, or the sword. Now Paul goes into the nebulous, ambiguous, indeterminate area of our knowledge and beyond. If you want to get scientific then he says not the troposphere, not the stratosphere, not the mesosphere, not the thermosphere, not the exosphere, and not the ionosphere. If you want to get practical: not what you can see or not see, not death or life, neither height nor depth, and not anything that has ever been created!

Let's clear something up. Let's be very biblical in understanding the spiritual dark world. It's powerful. What is going on here is that there is a mounted attack from the enemy where he wants to separate you from God. He wants to intervene and get you to think about other stuff. When you think about other stuff, you will be separated from God. But the enemy cannot stand up to our God. Yet we have this tendency to either ignore Satan or give him too much credit. Listen to what I am saying here: we base our spiritual decisions mostly on some feeling we have. But hear caution, caution, caution — feelings will get you in trouble in your spiritual life. Many times I don't feel like doing most things God wants me to do. And instead I feel like doing my own thing. A lot of times, a lot of us feel like God is not there, and it's then that you have to believe in Romans 8:38-39: NOTHING SEPARATES YOU from the love of God in Christ Jesus. It is so sad to think this way.

Here's the issue: Life happens, troubles come our way, disaster strikes, woes dominate daily, burdens burden us, pain pains us — and here's what happens in our relationship with God:

- Detachment
- Division
- Disjointedness
- Alienation

- Splitsville
- Divorce
- Secession
- Disconnection

I got disconnected from someone the other day when talking on the phone and I said, "They'll call me back... no worries." Or when people have a different political view from me I might say, "they're disconnected." We get disconnected from God and we don't panic anymore like we used to. The world is disconnected. That's so sad. Jesus came to connect us.

I have done a few funerals recently, and I always want to use those opportunities to connect people to reality. There's no better time to tell people that they are going to die and go to hell without Christ than at a funeral. Let me tell you the reason why. We have become so immune, apathetic, and non-responsive to death these days that we've become stoic, fatalistic, and resigned to whatever happens to people! Peruse the papers and social media and you will find that when a person dies these days it's "let's have a party!" Let's celebrate their life. Don't get me wrong. I am not against celebrating someone's life. But God intended mourning to be mourning. When someone dies, you cry. You don't raise a glass of Jim Beam in their honor. When someone dies before their time, you take inventory of your life and think, "What if that were me? What does God have for my life?" Not "Get a cheese tray from the Fresh Market and a box of wine!" What are we thinking?

So when I do a funeral, I preach the Gospel. I may preach peace, and hope, and love in Christ, but I also preach that sin does indeed separate us from God! Paul is talking to believers here. He is talking to those of us who have turned to Him and are in a relationship with Christ. And we are close to Him, so close that we are in Him and the Holy Spirit in us.

We love technology. Did you hear that Apple is now a $2 trillion company? Thanks to you and me. We love the convenience of communication and research and playing online and talking to our friends, but we absolutely hate the battery life of our technology. We hate it. You have to charge it. And if that weren't enough, sometimes you are not in your car or at home, and your phone needs charging. And why do they put only two outlets at each terminal at the airport? Everybody has a phone and everybody needs it to be charged. I can fix the world here: put one at every seat!

Like you, I have a charging cord beside my bed, and I bought the short one instead of the long one. You buy the long cord and you may be able to stretch it all over the place, but what do you do with all that extra? So, I got a short one this time and guess what? It's too short for me to charge my iPad while leaning it up beside the bed. So I have to get up, position it just right on my nightstand, and let it charge. And I can't tell you how many times my iPad charge gets to that screen where it says 10% battery life left, and then two minutes later, 5% battery life. Then right in the middle of a game I'm watching on my device, the screen goes blank. Can't we see that even technology tells us we need to be connected? (Thank you to the person who bought a long charger cord and shipped it to me after they heard this message!) Jesus said:

> *Abide in me, and I in you. As the branch cannot bear fruit by itself, unless it abides in the vine, neither can you, unless you abide in me. I am the vine; you are the branches. Whoever abides in me and I in him, he it is that bears much fruit, for apart from me you can do nothing. If anyone does not abide in me he is thrown away like a branch and withers; and the branches are gathered, thrown into the fire, and burned. If you abide in me, and my words abide in you, ask whatever you wish, and it will be done for you.*
>
> *-John 15:4-7*

If we call ourselves Christ followers and we do not abide in Him, to live in Him and to live for Him, then we are disconnected. And if we are disconnected, we can't do anything for God. You may think you do, but you don't. Jesus says, in essence, if you are disconnected long enough then it's like you were never connected.

And if you were never connected, you are to be thrown away… burned.

Maybe you are disconnected today. Maybe you feel like you are separated from God and about to get a divorce from Him and you need to be recharged. You need to be reconnected. How do I get there?

> *Oh, taste and see that the Lord is good! Blessed is the man who takes refuge in him! Oh, fear the Lord, you his saints, for those who fear him have no lack!*
>
> *The young lions suffer want and hunger; but those who seek the Lord lack no good thing. Come, O children, listen to me; I will teach you the fear of the Lord.*
>
> *What man is there who desires life and loves many days, that he may see good?*
>
> *Keep your tongue from evil and your lips from speaking deceit.*
>
> *Turn away from evil and do good; seek peace and pursue it.*
>
> *-Psalm 34:8-14*

- Taste & See

Tell me, when was the last time you got involved? I'm telling you this: don't fall for the enemy's lie that online church is your way to connect. It's not. Don't let technology fool you into thinking it's the way of the future. It's not. These are difficult times and we are doing our best, but online church is definitely *not* the way to go. The church was always intended to set up hors d'oeuvres of welcome to everyone, leading up to the main course of the Gospel, finished off with the dessert of the banquet table of the marriage supper of the LAMB! How do I taste? Taste, in order to recharge, by:

- Serving
- Giving
- Loving
- Joining
- Committing

Do these things, and you will connect, reconnect and become charged up! The church is about doing and ministering, not about feeling. You will never feel it first. Never! You are missing it by coming to church and sitting and soaking up a little only to have others squeeze it out of your life during the week. The Psalter says plainly to taste and see that God is good. He also says to do this if you feel separated:

- Seek & Fear
Every now and then, I don't know if it's because I bought the cheap cord, but every now and then it

doesn't connect properly to my device. It looks like it connects, but if improperly plugged in it doesn't charge. In order for you and me to be connected to God properly there has to be regular seeking and fearing of God. What does that look like? The Psalter tells us!

> *I will teach you the fear of the Lord. What man is there who desires life and loves many days, that he may see good? Keep your tongue from evil and your lips from speaking deceit. Turn away from evil and do good; seek peace and pursue it.*
> *-Psalm 34:11-14*

- Tame the Tongue

My goodness, if we could just learn to control our tongues, James tells us. Our mouths get us into so much trouble. And now – now – in our "woke" society, in our social distancing society, in our PC society, our vocabulary is limited. You better get control of your tongue brother, you better learn how to stop talking so much, sister. When you get close to God you learn that there is not a lot of talking to do, but a lot of listening! Fear of God means listening to God. Listening to God means staying in His Holy Word.

- Turn from Evil

Jesus says, "Slapped? Turn the other cheek." There's not a sermon to be preached. Stay away from bad stuff. He doesn't say run with your tail between your legs. He says if you are met with evil, then you respond in love:

> Let what you say be simply 'Yes' or 'No'; anything more than this comes from evil. "You have heard that it was said, 'An eye for an eye and a tooth for a tooth.' But I say to you, Do not resist the one who is evil. But if anyone slaps you on the right cheek, turn to him the other also.
>
> -Matthew 5:37-39

- Do Good

If you have to know what doing good is, then you are way too disconnected.

- Pursue Peace

I'm not talking about the hippie movement. So many people don't know what biblical peace is all about. It's so sad — Spiritually Obtuse Separation Anxiety Disorder. You may have SO SAD if you don't know Christ fully and completely as you should. It means in this world today you are not connected to God. You've let the world dictate to you that you don't care, and you don't know how to connect or reconnect. The answer is Jesus.

>Johnny's little sister, Cindy, got the same disease that Johnny had miraculously recovered from a few years earlier. The doctor said, "Cindy needs a transfusion and the only rare blood we can find is Johnny's." They asked Johnny about the transfusion. His lips quivered as he hesitated and then said, "Yes, I will."
>
>The day of the transfusion came, and they put Johnny and Cindy side by side on beds and hooked everything up. Johnny's smile faded when the needle pinched his skin. He lay there and watched the blood fill the tube, and then Johnny asked, "How long before I die?"

Johnny had no idea that transfusion just meant giving some blood. However, Jesus didn't hesitate, and He knew the blood He gave meant His death on a Cross. He has connected with us in the most supreme way, in the most loving way, in the only way. Will you connect to Him by giving Him your life in return? For those in Christ, there is no condemnation and no separation. Romans 8 is the greatest chapter in the Bible because it proclaims the greatest gift given to us from our great God.

The great chapter eight of Romans has been a magnificent study. Continue on it, memorize the verses, meditate upon them, let them saturate your heart and comfort you while you grow in Christ. When you do, you will discover how it just may be the greatest chapter to add to your life.

About the Author

Pastor Greg Dowey is the Founding and Senior Pastor at Fresh Church in Chapin, SC. His commitment to Christ, to Fresh Church, and to the Fresh Church family is indisputable. His heart's desire is to see people come to salvation in Christ and grow to maturity in Him. Pastor Greg emphasizes the importance of studying and living by God's Word. His unique weekly messages are biblically-based, and always relevant.

Pastor Greg was born on the United States Naval Base in Puerto Rico and grew up in Columbia, SC. He has pastored in the state of South Carolina for nearly 30 years.

Pastor Greg completed his undergraduate study at the University of South Carolina. Along with receiving his Masters of Divinity from Southwestern Theological Seminary in Fort Worth, Texas, he did additional post-graduate work at St. George's College in Jerusalem. He holds a Doctorate of Ministry from North Greenville University.

He and his wife Missie live in Irmo with their two Boston Terriers, Racket and Dixie. Their son, Jack, lives in Indianapolis where he is employed by the national headquarters of his fraternity.

Pastor Greg is an avid reader and aspiring writer. He enjoys sports and fitness, runs every day, and plays the occasional round of golf.

He and Missie are the founders of Simple Ministries, an international charity which provides bibles free of charge worldwide to people hungry for God's Word.

You can read Pastor Greg's blog at gregdowey.com. For more information about Simple Ministries, visit provesimple.com.

Acknowledgements

I want to thank my beautiful and lovely wife, Missie, for her artistic design and collaboration on this project. She provides a plethora of suggestion and is a treasure of wisdom. There is no better description of her than Proverbs 31– she is more precious than jewels.

Many thanks go to Karen Hulvey for editing this book. She works tirelessly combing through my manuscripts, repeatedly checking grammar, and making tremendous recommendations for clarity. She is also a joy to the church and in the work of the Lord Jesus!

And, thank you to FRESH Church for allowing me this opportunity… we are going deeper in order to go further!

RIGHTEOUS✺ACTS

Righteous Acts Publishing (RA) was established to print doctrinally sound books and materials for the purpose of maturing Christ-followers. This book is the inaugural introduction in this God-rich endeavor. With a high regard and view of Holy Scripture, RA stands on the inerrancy and sufficiency of God's Word. Realizing an ever-changing cultural shift to a more post-modern world, it is essential that the church hears an unadulterated, biblically based, and precision-minded Gospel message. The church is desperate to know the fear of God. Our goal is for the modern ecclesiastical community to comprehend the purity of the Gospel and hold on tightly to the call of the Lord Jesus to make disciples. We are committed to expository teaching, maintaining the supremacy of Christ, acts of serving in goodness, and living in righteousness.

"Who will not fear, O Lord, and glorify your name? For you alone are holy. All nations will come and worship you, for your righteous acts have been revealed." -Revelation 15:4

Made in United States
Orlando, FL
25 April 2022

17187958R00121